LIFELINES

Libertarian Education is a small independent publishing collective, which for the past quarter of a century has been campaigning for the development of non-authoritarian initiatives in education.

Also in this series:

Free School: The White Lion Experience, by Nigel Wright, ISBN 0-9513997-1-3

Freedom in Education: A do-it-yourself guide to the liberation of learning, ISBN 0-9513997-2-1

No Master High or Low: Libertarian Education and Schooling, 1880 - 1900, by John Shotton, ISBN 0-9513997-3-X

Real Education: Varieties of Freedom, by David Gribble, ISBN 0-9513997-5-6

The Dredd Phenomenon: Comics and Contemporary Society, by John Newsinger, ISBN 0-951-3997-7-2

Leave me alone, by Joanna Gore, ISBN 0-9513997-8-0

For the latest information about Libertarian Education, see http://www.libed.org.uk

LIFELINES

David Gribble

Libertarian Education

Published by:
Libertarian Education,
84b Whitechapel High Street, London E1 7QX

ISBN 0-9513997-9-9

Copyright: David Gribble and Libertarian Education, 2004

Cover design by Jayne Clementson
Photograph by courtesy of Moo Baan Dek

The photographs in the chapter on the Barns Experiment are reprinted with permission from the collection held by the Planned Environment Therapy Trust. The photographs of the Doctor Albizu Campos High School are by David Gribble. The photographs of Moo Baan Dek were provided by Moo Baan Dek itself. The photographs of Butterflies are by Lynette Gribble.

Printed and bound by:
Short Run Press, 25 Bittern Road, Sowton Industrial Estate, Exeter EX2 7LW. (Tel: 01392 211909)

To the many people of all ages who welcomed Lynette and me into their schools and organisations, talked to us, translated for us and explained to us, I dedicate this book with gratitude and affection.

CONTENTS

Acknowledgements

With regard to the Pedro Albizu Campos High School, Moo Baan Dek and Butterflies I would like to say thank you to all the people, of all ages, who have made it possible for me to write this book by their friendliness, openness and generosity with their time. Their names appear in the text, and to pick out individuals would be invidious.

Most of the information about David Wills and the Barns Experiment comes from the archives of the Planned Environment Therapy Trust, and I am grateful to Craig Fees and the Trustees for permission to make use of it.

David Gribble

Introduction

The kind of education that I have learnt to value over the last seventy years is described as, among other things, progressive, free, child-centred, democratic, liberal or non-authoritarian. Any one of these words on its own is either too narrow or too broad, but I can't write the whole list every time, so I shall fall back on the word "non-authoritarian".

My own schooling was of the opposite kind, and at the beginning of my career as a teacher I tried, rather unsuccessfully, to deal with children as I had been dealt with. Finally, after three years in one school, having become disillusioned with the petty discipline, the corporal punishment, the authoritarian hierarchy even among the staff and the impenetrable social barriers between adult and child, I gave in my notice before I had found another job.

By chance I came across an account of an entirely different style of education at Dartington Hall School. I wrote to the school; there happened to be a relevant vacancy; I was called for interview and I was offered the job. At Dartington there were no petty disciplinary issues and no corporal punishment. Social equality between adults and children was taken for granted. Decisions about the running of the school were taken at weekly meetings attended by all the children and staff who wished to do so; each person present had one vote.

I stayed at Dartington for almost thirty years, and when it was closed I was one of the founders of Sands School, which takes some of the principles of Dartington even further.

My experiences convinced me that non-authoritarian methods are successful, but, as those who opposed non-authoritarian methods often pointed out, what I had seen proved very little. At Dartington and Sands the children came from families who were, for the most part, themselves non-authoritarian and from the liberal middle class. For the working class, I was often told, such methods would be a disaster. Children who were unused to a non-authoritarian approach would never be able to make sensible decisions and govern their own lives wisely when they were left free to do so; any such idea was sentimental Rousseauism, a noble savage fallacy, Wordsworthian happy shepherd-boy naivety. A. S. Neill himself, it was pointed out, thought it would be mad to set up a Summerhillian school in a working-class area.

Since my retirement in 1991 I have visited non-authoritarian schools all round the world and in 1998 the first book about my experiences was

1

published. It is called *Real Education: Varieties of Freedom*, and it includes descriptions of eighteen different schools. There are two state schools with the ordinary local intake, a school in Japan for school-refusers, two schools in desperately poor areas in rural India and a school in Switzerland for children rejected even by other special schools. Wherever I went, however remote the culture from my own, I found a similar atmosphere of trust between adults and children.

I saw how successful these places were, but those criticisms I mentioned earlier still worried me. I wanted to investigate places that worked with children who faced other kinds of social difficulty. Ideally I wanted to find places that had not been set up with some particular philosophy in mind, but had developed naturally in response to particular problems. I chose four examples with this end in mind.

The first was the Barns Hostel, near Edinburgh. It was run during the Second World War by David Wills, a Quaker, for evacuees so disturbed or disruptive that no ordinary family could be asked to take them in.

The second was the Doctor Pedro Albizu Campos Puerto Rican High School, in Chicago, where a high proportion of the local teenagers, both boys and girls, are part of a gang society where rapes and killings are commonplace.

I visited Moo Baan Dek, in Thailand. Moo Baan Dek means "Children's Village", and in this village there are a hundred and fifty children and young people from backgrounds of the utmost poverty who have been abandoned, orphaned or abused. Moo Baan Dek is my third example.

Finally I went to see the Butterflies organisation, in Delhi, which offers non-formal education to street and working children, and helps them to understand and to assert their rights.

I hoped to find evidence that non-authoritarian education is suitable for children even from backgrounds like these.

David Wills and the Barns Hostel

A violent disciplinarian

I have chosen the story of David Wills and his work at the Barns Hostel for three reasons. Firstly, it illustrates the success of non-authoritarian methods with disadvantaged and disturbed children; secondly, it shows that such methods are not a refuge for weak staff who cannot manage such children by exerting normal discipline (a common misunderstanding among defenders of conventional education); and thirdly, David Wills supports his methods with strong arguments.

He was born in 1902 and brought up as a Baptist by a gentle mother and a harsh father. He was taught to keep out of fights, but he learnt to box in the Scouts. He left school when he was fourteen to become an office boy, but continued his studies at night school. Two or three years later, when he had a choice between becoming Assistant General Secretary to the YMCA in Norwich and taking a better-paid job as a salesman travelling in snuff, he chose the job which involved working with young people.

When he arrived in Norwich he found that as well as his secretarial work he had to run the Red Triangle Club. This was a boys' club set up by his predecessor, C. J. Marfleet, which was run as a broadly egalitarian, self-governing democracy.

He did not understand how to behave in this situation, and occasionally disciplinary problems arose. When he discussed these with some of the older boys, all they could say, rather unhelpfully, was that that sort of thing hadn't seemed to happen in Mr. Marfleet's time. Years later Wills realised that the boys felt not only respect for Marfleet, but also affection, a natural response to the affection which he evidently felt for them. As yet Wills still assumed that he ought to be able to make boys obey him, and he could not understand how Marfleet had succeeded.

There was a change in the leadership of the Norwich YMCA and the new man told Wills he was inexperienced and ignorant of the nature of boys, and should go to remedy these inadequacies at the Wallingford Farm Colony, and there he duly went, at the age of nineteen.

This institution had originally been set up to train tramps and down-and-outs in farming, so that they could be deported to the dominions. It later developed a section for boys and young men. The staff were known as Brothers, and were each responsible for a group of eight colonists. The idea

3

was a good one, but, as will be seen, the relationship was generally far from brotherly.

David Wills' first impressions were appalling. "The colonists," he wrote in his autobiography, "were the wildest, dirtiest, most depraved and degenerate set of mortals that I had ever seen, or have ever seen since, and all were dressed in stinking, moleskin trousers and jackets." The food was inadequate and disgusting – slices of bread were known as "mouldies", and the sausages they were served on Sundays were called "dead Dicks".

He was assigned to the section for adolescent boys and went through an exaggerated version of the hell familiar to every teacher who ever has tried to cope with out-of-control children within an authoritarian system.

On his first day he had to take his team out hedge-trimming. They showed him how it was done, cut enough to make a bonfire and then stood round, warming themselves. After a while Wills suggested that they should start work again, but they didn't move. Eventually he ordered one of the boys to pick up his hook and start cutting. The boy challenged Wills to hit him, and Wills said he had no intention of hitting anyone. This was a mistake. From then on he had no authority at all. "In less than a week," he wrote, "I was reduced to a state of despairing terror. The overwhelming relief when each day ended was equal only to the sickening fear with which I faced a new one. I could do nothing with my boys – and they could do what they liked with me."

When he was in charge of the dining room there was chaos. One day, in an attempt to exert his authority, he sent the mouldies back to the kitchen. The chaos redoubled, and was only stopped when a Brother known as Boxer arrived; as soon as Boxer entered the dining-room there was instant quiet.

Wills asked him for advice, and he suggested that he should buy himself a whistle. This advice he took, but between his lips a whistle was useless. "It seemed terribly unfair to me," wrote Wills, "that what was difficult for me almost to the point of impossibility, should be so absurdly easy to Boxer."

Boxer, as his nickname suggests, was a skilful and savage hitter. Wills resolved that he would acquire equal control, and asked for a transfer to a different home within the camp. With a fresh start he was sure he could make himself respected and feared, even if he was not liked. To be swiped by Boxer was a privilege to boast about, and that was the goal he set himself. One of his first moves in his new territory was to institute a fine for any boy who wore boots into the dormitory. Fifteen boys broke this rule during the first week, and he gave them their weekly envelopes of pocket money with small cards explaining that the fines had been deducted. The boys returned these cards to him, pasted on the door of his cubicle. He peeled them off the door and called the boys to him one at a time. As each boy came in he held out the card with his right hand, saying "Yours, I believe?" and as the boy reached to take it he hit him hard on the side of the head with his left.

He found satisfaction in taking this kind of violent revenge on his tormentors. He was called "Woodbine", after Wills Woodbines, the cheap cigarettes, and that infuriated him. On one occasion he chased a boy who provoked him in this way for three hundred yards, and when he finally caught him, punched him in the neck. When he wrote about this incident many years later, he described the sickening glee he felt as he punched.

He finally won the boys' respect after a boy with a club foot had been set up to call in through a window, "Come outside and get me, Goldflake." He went outside and hit him, and was jeered at as a coward for hitting a cripple. He offered to fight anyone else, and the colonists went to fetch their toughest representative. While they waited for their champion they stood round him in a square, chanting and throwing stones and bits of brick. The fight, when the champion arrived, was long and inconclusive. Wills' boxing skill enabled him to knock his opponent down over and over again, but the young man's sheer toughness kept him going until Wills was nearly exhausted. Finally the fight was stopped by the arrival of another Brother.

Wills may not have won the fight, but nevertheless he had proved himself to the colonists. He had a black eye, so he chose *Abide with me* as the evening hymn, and was able to share the boys' enjoyment of the line, "Hold thou thy cross before my closing eyes."

He delighted in his new-found power. One opportunity for displaying it was the distribution of the linen on Friday evenings. He required silence during Friday supper beforehand, and on one occasion, when a boy tried to carry more mugs than Wills had decreed, he knocked him down, cocoa and all. After supper and prayers the boys waited in silence while he whispered their names, one at a time, and they came to collect their new sheets. The whole process entailed what seemed to Wills a rapturous hour of perfect silence.

He was now plainly a successful staff member in a highly punitive authoritarian system. He became known as Basher Wills. He was even able to rescue another Brother in the same way as Boxer had rescued him. Mr. Low, several years his senior and a confirmed basher himself, had presumably committed some injustice that the boys found completely unacceptable, and had been attacked by a mob and forced to the ground. All Wills had to do to stop the attack was to make his presence known.

In his autobiography Wills describes his pleasure in his new power:

It gave me a great thrill to stand there among that mob that had so terrified and fascinated me two years ago, to rap on the table with the tin mug, and then to wait in tense and nervous expectancy to see what the response would be. Silence.

Basher Wills had achieved his ambition. He was successful within the system – one of the most successful on the entire staff. And yet before long he came to reject it utterly.

He did not change his mind because he was too weak to assert his authority over young people and felt he had to look for an alternative. He changed his mind because, in spite of his evident strength and success, he saw that the whole system was wrong.

He became aware, for instance, that both he and even Boxer were easily reduced to panic at the slightest sign of indiscipline. When there was a murmur as Boxer was about to say grace one day, Wills noticed that he was so frightened that he could not even remember the words of the grace, words that he had either heard spoken or uttered himself day after day for years. After a short period of baffled silence, all he could do was to growl, "Sit down!"

There was one boy who Wills never hit, a boy who seemed to him to be particularly well-behaved and pleasant. When he wrote about him he gave him the name of Charles. He took care not to treat him any differently from the others, but they both recognised a bond of affection. One day when Charles returned from work in the evening he appeared to have been crying. Wills asked what had happened and was told that Mr. Low had punched him. Wills was furious, and stormed off to pick a fight with Low. Luckily he did not find him. He went back and asked Charles what had happened, and the boy admitted that he had been insolent. When Wills later asked Low why he had punched him, he was shocked by the level of the insolence and realised that he would have reacted in the same way.

This was a moment of revelation. It occurred to Wills that some of the boys he punched probably had the respectful and friendly relationship with other staff members that he himself had with Charles, and that, where such a relationship existed, violence was as unnecessary as it was repugnant. The mere exertion of authority may result in temporary obedience, but nothing more. Affection, on the other hand, entails a desire to please. At last he began to understand Marfleet's success at the Norwich YMCA.

Another insight came from his observation of a Brother known as Jonah. Jonah was helpful and relaxed, neither a particularly good nor a particularly bad disciplinarian. He never hit any of the colonists, and it occurred to Wills that this was because, unlike Wills and Boxer, he was not frightened of them. Jonah's relationship with the children, Wills could not help acknowledging, was more Christian than his own.

His rescue of Mr. Low also gave him food for thought. Mr. Low, a basher and his senior, was less respected than he was. If the two of them were bashers, and one more successful than the other, perhaps it was not readiness to bash that gave influence over the boys, but some other quality. He had always supposed that it was his bullying ways that gave him ascendancy, but

Low was a worse bully than he was, and yet not always able to control the boys. It followed that bullying was ineffective, and therefore unnecessary.

The difference between himself and Low, Wills suspected, was that in spite of his aggressive ways he had come to respect the boys as individual people, whereas Low still saw them as a mob of cattle.

At about this time he became friends with C. V. S. Payne, a self-educated young man who was working in a separate part of the Colony, a mile or so away, where he cared for young people described as "odd cases and mental defectives". He had been gaoled as a conscientious objector during the war, had met Quakers in prison and had himself become a Quaker.

Wills and Payne met frequently, and talked about poetry and psychology, the boys and the Colony. It was Payne who first suggested to Wills that the reason for the colonists' behaviour might well be that they had never experienced the love that is vital if a healthy personality is to develop. Together they developed the idea that the one essential in their dealings with the kind of people they were concerned with at Wallingford was an attitude of unswerving, unconditional, unshakeable affection. What is more, they agreed that this was not in order to attain some end that seemed desirable to them, but because it was without question the will of God.

On the advice of another Brother, Wills left the Wallingford Farm Colony and went to Woodbrooke Quaker Study Centre, where he became a Quaker, read the works of Homer Lane and found support for all these new ideas.

He visited America, returned to work with miners in South Wales and then spent a period as a member of the staff in a borstal. From 1936 until the beginning of 1940 he ran the Hawkspur Camp for the training of wayward adolescents, where he was able to put into practice the ideas he had developed with C. V. S. Payne. The war came, and when the opportunity arose in 1940 he left Hawkspur and he and his wife Ruth went to become warden and matron of the Barns Hostel for unbilletable evacuees from Edinburgh.[1]

A School for Bad Boys

When I visited the Manor valley, where Barns House is situated, fifty-five years after the hostel had closed, there was very little memory of it, but most of those who did remember anything remembered it as "the school for bad boys." Robert Barr, the one local farmer who had been living in the area at the time, denied this, and said he believed "difficult boys" to be the proper

1   Most of the biographical detail in this section is taken from Wills'
    unpublished autobiography, held at the Planned Environment Therapy
    Trust Archive and Study Centre in Gloucestershire.

interpretation. They were boys, he said, who needed some personal attention that they had not had in their homes.

Mrs. Finnie, who had been the daughter of the gamekeeper at Barns during the war, was one who remembered the reputation of the hostel as a school for bad boys, but she too rejected this description. "They weren't bad as far as I was concerned," she said. She never knew them to get into any trouble while they were there, apart from disturbing the pheasants, and for this she was inclined to blame the staff rather than the children. When the house was returned to its owners in 1945, she went up with her parents to look round, and was surprised to see the drawing-room walls painted with murals by the boys, showing paratroopers and battles.

Almost all schools which allow their pupils an unusual degree of autonomy are regarded with mistrust in their immediate locality. Jürg Jegge, the brilliant Swiss educator, says he was thought of as the worst teacher in the Canton of Zurich. Countesthorpe College, in Leicester, in spite of eliminating truancy and achieving unusually good exam results, was harried by the local newspaper until the education authority appointed a head who introduced a more conventional atmosphere and truancy revived. It is not surprising that a hostel specifically set up to house children with social problems should have been regarded with suspicion.

It all started in November 1939, when Miss A. S. MacDonald, of the Scottish Society of Friends, wrote to the Department of Health proposing the establishment of what she called an Evacuation Camp. There are suggestions in the letter that the Quakers already had David Wills in mind – the use of the word "camp", for example, which may have arisen from the name of the Hawkspur Camp, where he was still working, and an unexplained sentence which read, "We feel we can state that we shall be able to find a suitable warden."

Other conditions were that it should involve camping and an outdoor life, it should aim for permanence, it should be for at least fifty children, it should have space for gardening and exercise, and it should be for children from nine to fourteen (the school-leaving age). "Our chief aim in establishing such a Camp School," the letter stated, "would be as a preventive measure, as it may help boys over a difficult period with suitable work."

The Evacuation Camp in the end never had more than thirty boys at any one time, but David Wills did agree to become its warden. In March 1940 a Department of Health official drove Miss MacDonald and others down to visit Barns House as a possible site for the Camp, and Miss MacDonald wrote to David Wills with this enthusiastic description.

This house seems to be perfect for our purpose. It lies in the valley of the Tweed, 100 yards from the banks. It is well-built and was occupied by the last tenant up to a year last December. It has been kept well-fired since. It has central heating and electric light, is in excellent condition and most of the windows have shutters. There are a number of bathrooms and excellent cupboard accommodation. The kitchen range is old but the Department will give us an adequate cooking range. There is accommodation for about 40 boys. There is also good accommodation for the Warden and his wife, and also the staff. There is about 3 to 4 acres of grassland belonging to the house, a splendid vegetable garden with fruit trees of about an acre and in good condition. A gardener belonging to the Estate attends to it and heats the house. There is a fine steading with a garage which could take four cars, so this suggests the size. There is a good deal of odd accommodation about this steading in excellent condition including a neat cottage with kitchen, bathroom, two bedrooms, electric light.

The building was taken over by the Government in exchange for rates, taxes and general upkeep, and a complicated financial arrangement was set up by which the Department of Health paid for expenses, Peeblesshire County Council paid for the salaries of the domestic staff, the Quakers paid Wills' salary and the Edinburgh Education Authority paid for the school equipment and the one teacher who was to be provided.

The hostel opened as a war emergency on July 1st 1940, a refuge for evacuees whose behaviour made it impossible for them to be billeted with families in the ordinary way. The house was to be the boys' home, and a wooden building in the grounds was to be their school. The first teacher, appointed by the Edinburgh Education Authority without consulting David Wills, was Stephen Bathgate. He was a man recommended by the fact that he had read books by A. S. Neill, the head of Summerhill School, where the children called the staff by their first names, made their own rules and decided whether to go to class or not; unfortunately he found himself unable to apply what he had read. "He thought he was a disciple of A. S. Neill until he faced the Barns boys, and then he decided he wasn't," said Kenneth Roberton, one of the other members of the staff, when I met him in 2000. He fell back on the tawse, the leather belt that was the traditional method of discipline in Scottish schools. He kept one hanging behind his door, and he made use of it.

The evacuees themselves

This is Wills' list of the symptoms that led to the referral of the fifty boys who attended Barns during the five and a quarter years of its existence:

SYMPTOM	Number reported on referral	Number discovered subsequently	Total
Stealing; "dishonesty"; Housebreaking	22	9	31
Enuresis; Encopresis; "dirty habits"	5	16	21
Truancy	16	0	16
"Unmanageable"; "Wild"; "Self-willed"; "Beyond control"	14	0	14
General insecurity, picture-aggressiveness, irrational fears, etc.		12	14
Temper tantrums		10	13
Lying		4	7
Speech defects	1	3	4
Wandering	1	0	4
Destructiveness	1	2	3
Backward; Ineducable	2	0	2
Cruelty	2	0	2
Tardiness	2	0	2
Begging	1	0	1
Indecency	1	0	1
TOTALS	79	**56**	**135**

The Barns Experiment, p. 35

Wills comments, "There is here an accumulation of 135 symptoms distributed among fifty boys, and you might assume, therefore that everything has been here recorded that could possibly be described as a symptom. That is not the case at all. The symptoms shewn are all what might fairly be described as *major* symptoms, any one of which would call for special treatment, though they are not necessarily all symptoms which, taken by themselves, would have justified a boy being sent to Barns. I confess that in compiling the list of symptoms it was in some cases difficult to know where to draw the line." Backwardness, for example, he says was a symptom in the majority.

In a report for the *Scottish Council for Research in Education: Evacuation Survey*, written in 1942 and revised in 1943, Wills gave the following statistics:

> 55 boys have so far been admitted, of whom 31 are now in residence. Of the 55, 19 came from other billets, and the remaining 36 direct from Edinburgh. ... 18 of the 36 are known to have had Police court experience, and there may

be others. Most of the remaining 18 appear to have been evacuated to avoid the Court. Such words as "incorrigible," "dangerous" and "hopeless case" occur frequently in the referral reports.

The IQs of the 31 boys in the school had been measured, with the following results:

IQ		
70 - 79	8	boys
80 - 89	7	
90 - 99	13	
100 +	3	

I asked Kenneth Roberton if the boys ever talked about their old schools.

Never heard them mention schools. Bad, bad memories I should think, their schools, because they would all have been at the bottom of the class, quite unjustifiably, but they would have been bottom of a class of fifty kids, fifty or sixty which was quite a regular number in slum area primary schools in those days. They would get no education at all. The Scottish education system was excellent in producing the elite at the top, it produced more doctors, more philosophers than any other education system, but as for those lower down in the milk bottle, they didn't get any education at all, they got the tawse.

When I first looked at the list of symptoms I was inclined to notice those that seemed to offer little in the way of threat to others, such as speech defects, wandering and tardiness. It doesn't look too bad, I thought. And then I realised that, out of the fifty boys who attended the school at various times, fourteen were considered beyond control, that is to say more than a quarter of them. Thirty-one had probably committed criminal offences, though it is not clear quite what "dishonesty", sandwiched between stealing and housebreaking, actually means. Thirteen, another quarter, were given to temper tantrums. When I imagined trying to handle such a group, my heart sank. On top of this, fourteen were aggressive or irrationally fearful, twenty-one either had inadequate control over their bladders or bowels or else chose to excrete in inappropriate places (if I have correctly interpreted the term "dirty habits").

And when the first boys arrived and found that there was no system of punishment, they behaved as wildly and uncontrollably as the people who had referred them would have expected. This is David Wills's own account of what happened:

The chief game seemed to consist of charging wildly through the house howling madly and slamming all the doors on the way. Any kind of organised activity was almost impossible. Crockery would be dashed on to stone floors, games destroyed, furniture broken, stones hurled through windows. Mealtimes were an indescribable babel, and there were mass truantings from school.

The Barns Experiment, p. 11

The boys were waiting for the adults to impose discipline on them, and found them (apart from the schoolteacher) only patient, supportive and affectionate. This absence of punishment they found incomprehensible.

In the report to the Scottish Council for Research in Education, mentioned above, Wills gave a slightly different account of events.

During the first few months, as the first few batches of boys were finding their feet all together, there was a good deal of disorder. This had its culmination about the end of the third month when there was chaos, confusion and a good deal of rioting and window-smashing. Shortly afterwards the Christmas holidays started, and all the disorder was finished, it seemed, overnight.

The boys stayed at the hostel over the Christmas holidays. The difference was that they did not have to submit to the school-teacher's discipline every day. Wills does not make this connection himself, but it seems an important one.

The Theoretical Approach

No punishment

In their long discussions at the Wallingford Farm Colony, Wills and Payne had agreed that it was God's will that they should show affection towards children, and that one aspect of this duty was the rejection of the use of punishment. To the will of God, Wills added a sound practical justification.

1. It establishes a base motive for conduct.
2. It has been tried, and has failed; or alternatively, it has been so misused in the past as to destroy its usefulness now.
3. It militates against the establishment of the relationship which we consider necessary between staff and children – a relationship in which the child must feel himself to be loved.
4. Many delinquent children (and adults) are seeking punishment as a means of assuaging their guilt-feelings.
But that is not all; there is still another. When the offender has "paid for" his crime, he can "buy" another with an easy conscience.

The Barns Experiment, p. 22

The SCRE report mentioned yet another reason for avoiding punishment. I was surprised when I first read it, but on reflection I find it one of the most cogent. Punishment, said Wills, "shifts responsibility for behaviour onto the adult, instead of leaving it with the child."

Wills liked to tell the story of the time he found some boys helpfully stacking logs outside the back door. He asked them where they had found them, and they showed him an area next door to the playing field which had recently been cleared of trees. He carefully explained that the wood didn't belong to them, and the boys asked whether they would "get into a row". Oh no, he said, it might well be scrap timber, but the point was it didn't belong to them. He walked off, pleased with his gentle explanation, but when he passed by again a short time later the boys were still collecting more wood. He commented in some surprise that he had told them it was wrong to help themselves like that. "Oh no you didn't," they said. "You said it was all right to take it." Wills was flabbergasted, because they plainly believed they were telling the truth. They enlightened him: "You said we wouldn't get into a row."

If you have always been punished, even for minor offences, if you have been taught that if you do anything wrong you are certain to get into a row, then it follows that if you don't get punished, if you don't get into a row, then what you have done must be all right.

"I cannot feel I am overcoming evil with good," wrote Wills, "if I coerce a boy by means of corporal punishment – or any other kind of punishment – however successful it may at the moment appear. ... If punishment overcomes evil at all (which I do not for one moment believe) it has overcome it with evil, as I cannot believe that the deliberate infliction of pain (and not incidentally and unwillingly, as in the case of e.g., pulling out a tooth) is anything but evil." (**The Barns Experiment, p. 79**)

"The finest type of citizen," he also wrote, "is he who obeys no law blindly out of an unthinking respect for authority or fear of penalties; it is he whose conduct is based on a rational understanding of why a given type of behaviour is desirable, and who will persist in that type of behaviour whatever the consequences to himself." (**The Barns Experiment, p. 17**)

Shared Responsibility

"Shared responsibility" is Wills' term for what other institutions have usually called "self-government" or "democracy".

There must be order, says Wills, there must be a respected authority, even in a small community of forty persons. "But in order that there may be a minimum of misunderstanding and resentment, let us, so far as possible, make such rules as may be necessary *between us*, for the same reason. It may be found necessary for the common good – or even for the good of the individuals concerned, to prevent worse befalling them – to restrict the liberty of some, which may seem very much like punishing them. But if the decision is arrived at as the result of a discussion among his peers, he may at least understand the reason for it." **(The Barns Experiment, p. 81)**

This entails some form of meeting, where such matters can be discussed. At Barns many different systems evolved at different times, but they usually included a house meeting at least once a week for making general decisions, and a court for dealing with misdemeanours. Wills was clear that in areas where the meeting had jurisdiction, that jurisdiction must be absolute. "It is better," he said, "to limit the children's responsibility to something very small, if that authority is absolute, than to get them a wide but vague sphere of control with the danger that you might step in one day and veto a decision which they have made." **(The Barns Experiment, p. 59)**

At Barns, as will be seen, he allowed the children's authority to extend very widely indeed.

In *Spare the Rod*, his book about Bodenham Manor, where he worked after leaving Barns, he gives a full account of his reasons for believing shared responsibility to be "a very valuable instrument". Here is a slightly abbreviated version of this account.

(I) It is a natural vehicle for group therapy. ... [Group therapy] consists in essence of a discussion of a person's problems and difficulties by the group of which he is a member, the underlying assumptions being that (a) other people in the group may have had similar difficulties; (b) the recapitulation in conversation may have a certain abreactive value; (c) the patient may be more likely to accept views and remedies laid down by his peers than those laid down by a person in authority such as a "counsellor" or psychiatrist and (d) in the course of the discussions the psychiatrically trained counsellor has many opportunities both for gaining a better understanding of this client's difficulties and for putting in a word in season (directly or otherwise) towards their amelioration.

...

In these discussions there are frequent references not only to specific concrete things, but also to abstract ideas such as the desirability of everybody "helping the community", the fact that citizenship involves duties as well as rights, and so on. Often these sentiments are expressed by adults. They are rapidly picked up by any child who has "identified" with that particular adult and we hear children sometimes giving utterance to sentiments notably at variance with their conduct; but that doesn't matter because as a rule it is not hypocrisy or self-righteousness, but the expression of a standard which the child is in process of accepting as his own.

(II) Shared responsibility is a means by which the children may learn that socially acceptable behaviour is demanded of them not only as a result of adult prejudice, but also by their peers. ...

(III) Under shared responsibility the adults are less preoccupied with disciplinary matters than under a more orthodox regime and can therefore more easily maintain the friendly, affectionate relationship that is so necessary.

(IV) Side by side with the above is a little-recognised virtue of shared responsibility – that it enhances the authority of the adults. ... The fact that the adult so seldom says "Thou shalt not" or "Thou shalt" tends to make his authority more effective when he does. ...

(V) Shared responsibility is a device for encouraging and making constructive use of the herd instinct which in maladjusted children is apt to be either anti-socially directed or pathologically inhibited. ...

(VI) Shared responsibility helps to protect the weak and the small from the big and aggressive without the stigma of tale-bearing.

(VII) Shared responsibility satisfies the need that all children have to feel that their side of the question is being heard – that they are getting fair play.

(VIII) Shared responsibility is a means by which the child can be helped by practical experience to learn that laws exist for our mutual protection, and that the price of freedom is eternal vigilance – or in other words that if he wants the place to be a good place, he will have to make his contribution.

Love

First and foremost and all the time the children must feel themselves to be loved.

The Barns Experiment, p 60

For when I speak of love I do mean love – I mean the kind of feeling a parent has for his children. I do not mean the esteem which a child can earn from the adults in its environment by being 'a good boy'. I do not mean the benign and somewhat affectionate feeling that a teacher might feel for his class when everything is going steadily forward. The kind of thing I am thinking of has no relation to the behaviour of the child, and is not influenced by it. It cannot be bought with goodness nor lost by misbehaviour. ... It is not just a matter of being 'awfully fond of children'. Anyone can be that. It is a matter of being 'awfully fond' of Johnny Jones whose table manners are nauseating (he sits opposite you and crams as much food into his mouth as he possibly can; this he chews with his big mouth wide open; presently he lets out a loud guffaw, ejecting his breath powerfully through his overfull and open mouth ...); it is a matter of being 'awfully fond' of Willie Smith whose nose is usually in a condition such as to make one retch almost every time one sees it; it is a matter of being 'awfully fond' of Tommy Green, who has all these failings and a foul and nasty disposition thrown in. It consists of loving this Tommy Green in spite of all that, of making him feel that this affection is always there, is something on which he can absolutely rely, which will never fail, whatever he may do. It consists of establishing a relationship such that, however much the child may wound his own self-esteem, he cannot damage the esteem in which we hold him.

The Barns Experiment, p. 64.

Payne had first suggested to Wills that it was lack of love that was the major cause of all the disturbed behaviour shown by the colonists at Wallingford Farm Colony. At Barns Wills was determined that the boys in his charge, similarly deprived, should be compensated for that lack.

If I read all the books about psychotherapy and group therapy and every other kind of therapy and though I apply all the latest psychiatric and pedagogic methods, and have not love, I am nothing. All goes, said Barrie in a much quoted passage, if courage goes. All goes, say I, if love goes.

Spare the Rod, p. 44.

The Approach in Practice

I have emphasised the boys' behavioural problems because I wanted to make it plain that the staff faced considerable difficulties. Kenneth Roberton, however, has very positive memories of the beginnings of the hostel.

KR: *I can very well remember meeting and bringing to the house the first five boys. And they seemed quite at ease with me because I was at ease with them because I was expressing the philosophy of Barns already, because I was sympathetic to the philosophy of Barns. These boys came to us direct from Edinburgh – we were supposed to take difficult evacuees but by the time Barns had set up the countryside had rejected all the difficult evacuees, they were all back in Edinburgh, by that time. We only had two or three boys, I should think, who came from the reception area. These five little boys with their little attaché cases and their gas masks arrived straight from Edinburgh. Somebody must have put them on a bus – there must have been instructions that they were put on a bus at Peebles to go to Lyne Junction because it was difficult to get directly to Barns; Barns was on the wrong side of the river. The house stood on the Tweed, close to the Tweed, and on the other side a fieldwidth away was the railway line and the road, and you could only get to Barns by going a mile and a half to two miles beyond Barns in either direction. If you took the bus to Lyne Junction there, which these little boys did, then you had to walk to Barns, two miles, you could only come by foot. Otherwise you had to come over the bridge, there, and come back. I met them there and looking back on it now I seem to feel that they accepted me completely without any difficulty as a friend who'd come to meet them and was taking them to some nice place where they could be looked after, and we toddled along the two miles into*

Barns and the relationship was rapidly established – was already established, I think. It wasn't long before they started to call me Kenny.

DG: *Did they call David Wills David, as well?*

KR: *David? No, David was never called David. He was called Mr. Wills for a little time but very soon after he was called Willsy.*

DG: *It's very characteristic of that sort of place. Were they wild at the beginning, like at Bodenham Manor?*

KR: *No, they didn't – this kind of experience that apparently they had in Bodenham we didn't have at all. No. They settled in very comfortably, I think, and established a very good relationship with all the adults and – no, they weren't wild.*

DG: *Can you remember –*

KR: *Their language was frightful. And my dear English lover who later became my wife was astonished when she used to come and visit me at the stream of foul language that used to come from these little boys.*

How can this comparatively serene beginning be reconciled with Wills' description of smashed crockery, broken windows, truanting and the near impossibility of organised activity?

Quite easily. It is not only that Kenneth Roberton remembers the good times more clearly than the bad ones. It is also that a good relationship with adults and the occasional smashing of crockery are not incompatible. When you are dealing with boys with major problems there are bound to be outbreaks of rage or distress. In between those outbreaks there is time for affection and support.

The SCRE report offers an illustration:

> *The staff of Barns do not like bad language, and do not attempt to disguise their dislike of it. Nevertheless they do often feel that they are making real progress when a boy looks up from his pillow with an expression of trust and affection which is the true respect and, reverting to the language of the cradle, calls out "Goodnight, you old bugger."*

Wills did not say organised activity was impossible, he said it was *almost* impossible, and the person who had the most trouble was Stephen Bathgate, the authoritarian schoolmaster with his tawse. What sort of difficulty did he have, I asked Roberton.

KR: *They wouldn't do what he said. One day David came in and he told me that he'd stood outside the classroom and he'd heard pandemonium and he'd heard Stephen in his bull-like voice – he had a very bull-like physique and powerful voice, Stephen – say to these terrible little boys, "I'll give you three to be quiet." Pandemonium. "One. Two. Three. THREE!!" Still*

Barns boys with Kenneth Roberton

pandemonium. (Laughter) We made life difficult for Stephen. Not wittingly, but . . .

DG: *He had a different approach.*

KR: *Yes. Yes. The little boys that had become used to us, to Willsy and me and our attitude and the attitude of the women, and they'd become used to such strange remarks as Willsy, I can remember, making to one, one day. One of these little boys said "Fuck yourself, Willsy!" "Impossible, my dear boy," he said quite calmly, passing on. But Stephen of course would have reacted in a totally different way. He'd have reached for the tawse.*

DG: *Can you pinpoint any other differences between the way you behaved with the children and the way Stephen did? Because it must have been a very big difference, really.*

KR: *Yes, well, Stephen just wanted to impose the old-fashioned Scottish discipline, which was based quite simply on the tawse, and a very rigid idea of how little children should behave.*

Kenneth Roberton also told me about what he described as "the first absconding". This account illustrates both the so-called unmanageable behaviour of the boys, and the good relationships with the staff which gradually brought them round.

KR: *We suddenly discovered we had no boys. They're not here. It's dinner-time or something, and they're not here. And I went and looked for them. I surmised what way they would have gone. Eventually I did find them, they had not progressed very far. They had progressed no more than a mile or so, through the woods towards the road to Peebles. When I found them they more or less invited me to belt them. Well, they were sorry, they shouldn't have done this and I was wearing a belt, and I was supposed to take the belt off and punish them, and I said that that wasn't the idea at all. The idea was that I had found them, and I had come from what was their home, was our home as well, and I'd come to bring them back, if they would come back. So they all said they would come back. They just came back. That was the end of that absconding.*

DG: *What did they think? David Wills said that when he was at Wallingford Farm Col . . . when he was weak with the boys – they interpreted it as weak – the . . . . . . of him as stupid, and so he had to become violent in order to get his own way.*

KR: *Oh yes?*

DG: *So did the boys, when you didn't take off your belt and hit them, did they lose respect for you?*

KR: *No. No. No. They continued to consider that Willsy and Kenny could deal with all sorts of awkward situations, that Willsy and Kenny were a formidable combination.*

In his Warden's Report at the end of the first year Wills explained precisely how the hostel was handling the question of punishment.

No punishments are inflicted by the hostel staff, but the insistence on things being done in their proper order sometimes results in a kind of automatic sanction. Thus boots must be cleaned before washing, or a second wash may be necessary; beds must be made before breakfast, and breakfast cannot be kept waiting indefinitely. It is perhaps not casuistic to distinguish between this kind of thing and the arbitrary inflicting of a specially devised penalty for misbehaviour. Corporal punishment is avoided, but a staff member may use his superior strength to check a bully, or a boy who is being disorderly may be sent from a room.

A potent cause of misbehaviour in children is the absence of a sense of security owing to lack of affection in early years and to the irregular and irrational use of punishment. At Barns an attempt is made to supply the first lack, and to remove such insecurity as is associated with punishment by not using it at all.

Kenneth Roberton was only on the staff for one year. Wills wanted him kept on, and wrote to the managers, in the same Warden's Report as I have just quoted, "I consider it important to make every effort to retain Mr. Roberton. He is enthusiastic about the work, anxious to stay, and has an admirable way with children." However, he and his "dear English lover", who had been so astonished at little boys' streams of foul language, got married. "David tried to get her employed as the cook," Kenneth Roberton told me, "but somebody on the Management Committee apparently took the view that it was all very well tolerating conscientious objectors up to a point, but enabling them to live with their wives was another matter. They should not go out of their way to facilitate that. My sardonic remark on that was that as long as the conscientious objectors were living with their own wives they wouldn't be living with the soldiers' wives." Nevertheless Roberton had to go.

Shared responsibility was introduced gradually as the boys got used to the atmosphere and began to understand what was necessary to ensure a contented and smooth-running community. By the second year there was no longer any need for a Willsy and a Kenny to deal with disciplinary issues, and by 1944 Ben Stoddard, a young teacher who had taken over the schoolroom from the unsuccessful disciplinarian, described the following incident in his report on the school. (This was at a time when the boys were electing a President and a Vice President from among their number, who appointed a number of officers to make sure the school was running smoothly.)

Two boys waiting to have their work corrected started to fight over their position in the queue. The officer on duty found the task of stopping them beyond him. Several boys called out to me, "Why don't you stop them?" I replied that it was not my job; I was there to teach. They had undertaken to maintain order and now was their chance to do it. If I had been in charge this would never have happened, and so on. In the meantime several others had joined the tussle, so the officer called in the Vice President who ordered everyone back to their places and the originator out of the [classroom] altogether. It was a source of considerable satisfaction to me to see the boys accepting full responsibility, even in a crisis. C. Milligan afterwards said to me with a grin, "You're not a teacher, you're just a man."

You could hardly imagine anything more different from the behaviour of his bull-necked, tawse-wielding predecessor.

The actual system of government varied, but at the beginning the weekly house meeting made the rules, settled disputes and distributed jobs to be done. After a while the system seemed to be getting top-heavy with rules and regulations, and Wills therefore took over as dictator, as A. S. Neill once did at Summerhill, saying he would be ready and willing to hand over to anyone who would really run the place, from getting up to bedtime, seven days a week.

He was at first astonished at how easily the boys accepted his authority, but after only a week they called a meeting of all those who wanted to end the dictatorship. This is Wills' account of what happened.

About half the boys attended the meeting, and as I had made it clear that I should be glad to help in any way, I was invited and attended. Wally Straight (aged 12) was elected to the Chair, and opened the meeting with a few well-chosen words, of which the following is the official record: "The Chairman (Wally Straight) told the meeting that they now had an opportunity to organise Barns all over again, and to do things the way they wanted them done. He said that it was up to the meeting to prove that Barns' boys could look after themselves." (Oddly enough there is no record of who was appointed Secretary, and was therefore responsible for the admirable minutes, but I think it was Ted Bounce.)

Then I butted in and asked if I might say a few words. On permission being given, I reminded them that I was only going to surrender my authority to a properly constituted body that would really do the job, and explained what "the job" was. Then I said that one of the weaknesses of the House meeting had been that it was overweighted with adults so that some boys were reluctant to speak their minds. I didn't want the new thing to have the same disability, so I proposed to step outside, but if they wanted advice on any specific point they could call me in. Then I withdrew, though I have to confess that (as the meeting was in the Dining Room) I did a little eavesdropping through the lift hatch.

It was an extremely rowdy meeting and several boys were ejected for failing to respect the Chair. I was called in for advice on two or three points, withdrawing each time after I had said my piece.

Two or three meetings were necessary before everything was cleared up, and what came to birth was "The Citizens' Association." The name, I am sorry to say, was mine – they couldn't think of one themselves – but the constitution they evolved was entirely theirs.

The Citizens' Association might be described, in brief, as an oligarchy of the Elect. Membership was open to anyone who could "prove that he was willing to work for Barns." We were all frightfully excited and pleased about the new developments. I wrote several long letters to our Chairman, keeping her posted with the latest events. Reading them through to refresh my memory recalls very vividly the spirit and atmosphere of the time, and I think I cannot do better than quote from them. '... It was undoubtedly the most serious and purposeful meeting we have had here. The Citizens' Association took over forthwith. They put themselves to bed and supervised themselves in the bathroom. The following morning, Tuesday, my day off, sometimes known as "racket day", they got themselves up and did all that was necessary with no adult supervision at all, and May says the dormitories were cleaner than she has ever known them. The Chairman of the Citizens' Association took charge of the Dining Room, ringing the bell for Grace, and so on. And so they continued to bedtime, when they put themselves to bed. Everything did not go smoothly, by any means. There were various contingencies for which they had not legislated in advance; there were conflicting interpretations of such rules as had been made; some boys were jealous of those in office – and so on. But from all accounts it seems to have been as well-ordered and peaceful a Tuesday as we have had for some time.'

...

Membership of the Citizens' Association consisted at first of those who had attended the first meeting and had expressed their willingness to "help Barns" – there were thirteen of them. Thereafter, new members had to be nominated by a Citizen and approved by a majority of the Association. Every Citizen had to take his turn as "Officer on Duty", two being appointed for each day. The Officers on Duty were, in short, responsible for the orderly carrying out of the routine from rising in the morning until "Lights Out" at night. It was quickly recognised that the Officers on Duty were not exercising a personal authority, but were acting on behalf of the community as a whole, and we were amused as well as pleased to see that one of the smallest boys ... seemed to exercise greater authority than the biggest boy in the place.

The Barns Experiment, pp. 52 ff

The Citizens' Association lasted about eight months before being dissolved by common consent, and replaced by a cabinet system. At the weekly house meeting a Prime Minister was appointed, and he appointed Ministers of

Justice, Routine, Work, School and Money. As well as undertaking their individual responsibilities, they sat every day as a court. They received a salary of between threepence and sixpence; the funds to meet these salaries were raised by taxation – a halfpenny or a penny a week for children, and double that amount for adults.

Barns had several other systems, some better than others, but the Citizens' Association was the most remarkable in that it was devised completely by the boys. However, although the system of government was theirs, its purpose seems to have been to maintain the routine that had been originally established by the adults, including getting-up times and bedtimes, grace before meals and regular lesson times.

It is time, perhaps, to tell of the effects of the Barns regime on individual boys. I have failed to track down any of them, but there are some notes in David Wills' annual reports, and Kenneth Roberton told me of one boy who, when one of the others asked him what happened when he wet the bed at the convent where he had previously been billeted, replied, "I was thrashed by the holy nuns of Jesus." Surely Barns must have been a happy refuge for him.

Here are four sets of extracts from notes made at staff meetings, as presented by Wills in his annual reports. (Boy No. 1 and Boy No. 2 are from his first report, and the two "cases" from his second.)

Boy No. 1 (aged 9).
At 16/1/1941. – Apparently an incorrigible thief and liar – always stealing, hardly seems to know truth from falsehood. Loves screaming, and at bed-time makes himself difficult so that he has to be forcibly undressed, screaming all the time. Wall scribbler. Spits in people's faces. Language deplorable.

At 27/3/41. – Always engaged in some exciting activity, games, or mischief. Very busy and happy as a rule, but moody. Little evidence of stealing, except pencils.

At 25/6/41. – A happy child, presenting now no serious problems; but gains need to be consolidated.

Boy No. 2 (aged 11).
At 12/12/1940. – A sturdy little tough, looks as if high spirits and sense of fun may have been the main cause of trouble.

At 16/1/41. – Always sounds truculent. Damages boots and clothes deliberately. Offensive and aggressive in the extreme, especially to House Matron – kicks her and spits at her. Always looks worried.

At 12/6/41. – "A cherub." A very happy, attractive, cheerful little boy, though easily upset by unkindness, real or imagined.

Case No. 46

At 16/1/42. – A very stormy specimen. Fighting, quarrelling, etc. Very bright in school when he can be persuaded to go, or to do anything.

At 20/2/42. – Told J. P. he had tried to kill his mother with a knife, but only grazed her arm. Says he is going to be a tramp. Tried to set kitchen on fire by pouring paraffin on floor and setting light to it. Periods of maniacal violence every day, much smashing of crockery, throwing of knives, etc.

At 8/4/42. – Feeling much more secure now, much less often seeking punishment. Good general improvement. Goes to school without any difficulty. Is to be nominated for membership of Citizens' Association.

At 6/5/42. – Has been accepted as a member of the Citizens' Association, and has been made its Treasurer, which means a good deal to him. Improvement in general maintained, although he has had a little trouble this week.

Case No. 19

At 1/5/41. – He is abnormally childish, and must learn to accept responsibility.

At 18/6/41. – On 10th May, in company with —, stole some sweets out of —'s locker and hid them in playing field.

At 20/11/41. – Essentially a weak character. Has recently been concerned with — and — in a larder-raiding episode. Will probably have to get worse before he improves.

At 22/1/42. – A very difficult period, stealing, staying out after bedtime, etc.

At 26/2/42. – Early in the month, in company with —, attempted to break into a house on way home from pictures. This was followed by a visit from the police, but apparently there is to be no prosecution.

At 26/3/42. – General improvement seen. Recently appointed Secretary of Citizens' Association and carries out his duties conscientiously. Is developing a sense of responsibility.

At 29/4/42. – Is now Chairman of Citizens' Association. Conscientious, reliable. Easily best Chairman so far.

At 20/5/42. – Still a competent and courageous Chairman.

At 1/6/42. – Still Chairman – longest to hold office – but otherwise seems slightly "off the rails" lately. Less conscientious in carrying out his duties, is probably doing a little pilfering in the kitchen, and is being very difficult in school.

The great virtue of these reports is that they are notes from actual staff meetings, written to help the staff rather than to reassure outsiders. They show that even after the hostel had been in action for some time there were still instances of dangerous violence, criminal behaviour and relapses on the part of boys who had seemed to be doing well.

Reports from outsiders, and other objective evidence

Occasionally visitors to Barns wrote reports about their experiences. I quote here from three positive reports, and later from a negative one. First, a professional in the field, Frank Mathews:

> My visit to these two places [the other one was Dunnow Hall, Cheshire] was one of the three most interesting experiences in 50 years of social work.
>
> ...
>
> The outstanding thing about the Home is the happiness and the harmony that prevail. It is in fact entirely a home spelt with a small h. There is no trace of Institution about it. The staff and children are friends and equals.
>
> ...
>
> The first morning when I was standing in the porch after breakfast I was asked if I would like to see the pets and was introduced to a pigeon, a rabbit and a guinea-pig, and was shown how a tailless pigeon could fly. There was another pigeon which was not to be touched "because it had eggs in its belly." After this I was taken round the whole place and introduced to the gardener. The morning before I left one quite small boy asked me if I would like to see his picture book, which proved to be some political cartoons about Hitler – a group came round and explained to me all the funny points, in scotch so soft that I could hardly hear it and was quite unable to understand them, but I enjoyed it.
>
> ...
>
> There are no punishments but there are consequences – that is to say, if children make a row in the dormitories and disturb other children then the council sends them to bed early the next day so that they may not disturb others a second night. If they are noisy at meal times or like to eat their food in the same haphazard way they did at home, the council sends them to eat in another room until they feel they would like to return and eat their food with their fellows.
>
> ...
>
> The children have the free run of the whole place – kitchen, garden and staff room. They go in and out of the staff room as they like and listen to the wireless or gramophone, and take part in any discussion that is going on. Their ages are from 9 – 14 and I should judge that the average age would be about 11. There are no servants at all. The whole of the staff are cultured people. ... There is even no charwoman and a former teacher even doing some of the charring.
>
> ...
>
> I asked Mr. Wills how it was that difficult children did not quarrel? He said that when they quarrelled badly one of them would charge the other, or rather would threaten to charge him, before the children's council. This

immediately stopped the quarrel and more often than not the charge was forgotten before the council met in the evening.

H. A. Rees visited with a friend in June 1944:

When I saw them they were a contented though noisy lot, full of high spirits and with many different inclinations. My companion and I arrived there in the evening of an unusual summer day and the boys made a happy group on the steps before supper. Two boys came along and took our light bags and others came along spontaneously to greet us. We greeted them and chatted for a few moments before going inside. We did not see any more of the boys that evening as, just then, the supper bell was tinkled, calling them in. We did hear a little more of them getting rid of high spirits but, in a very short time after supper and ablutions, quiet descended.

...

The boys were a joy to see in the water. All their inhibitions apparently cast off they swam down the current and struggled back against it. A few who could not yet swim were diligently practising in a warm sandy backwater. Time passed all too quickly in swimming, eating and climbing trees for this happy crew and though some had gone back to the house earlier, either to do duties or from choice, the remainder were collected at about a quarter to seven to go back to the house, chattering happily in their broad scots about what happened to be uppermost in their minds at the moment. A small red-headed boy singled me out as a companion, pointing to the birds' nests he could see on the way. He was particularly clever at this and had won for himself quite a reputation as an authority on the natural life of the district.

...

[By the end of the second day] we were all firm friends.

And a Dr. Burns made an official report to the Finance and Executive Committee in December, 1943:

The staff are nine in number. Being all educated people the atmosphere of freedom and equality, not to mention fraternity, is easier to maintain, especially as they are all imbued with similar ethical ideas.

...

There was an order evident in the routine of the place which was largely independent of rules imposed from above and formed part of the spirit of the place.

...

I attended a meeting of the boys, with some of the staff, held to elect a President and various Ministers for different purposes such as Routine, Justice, Recreation, etc. This might seem, at first sight and hearing, to have been more of a game than a real effort of self-government, but it became apparent soon

An overloaded boat on the Tweed

27

after the meeting that the "officials" were really doing their jobs and that there was something real and valuable being effected.

The other records of Barns that are undeniably genuine, not angled to fit Wills' personal point of view, are the photographs. They were of course taken of selected scenes, but they show children and adults together in what are clearly typical situations, and they show boys standing, moving and playing with an unconstrained naturalness that cannot be simulated.

There are several photographs of informal groups on the front steps. One includes two of the women staff, each of whom has an arm round a boy on either side of her. There are shots of the boys playing naked in the river, with one staff member standing on the bank to supervise. In another swimming picture there is a woman in a bathing suit sitting on the pebbly shore; a small boy has his arm round her shoulder. There are five boys lovingly showing off their guineapigs; only one of them is looking at the camera: three of the others are more interested in one particular guineapig, and the fifth is hunching his shoulder to help the guineapig that is crawling round the back of his neck. There are boys passing equipment along a long line to load on to a cart, ready for camp. There are a man and nine boys standing on a boat that looks home-made; some of the boys are naked; they all look confident and happy. There are a few portraits of individuals, for instance the first boy chairman of the house meeting; he is wearing an open-necked shirt and baggy shorts; he has a confident, natural expression and feels no need to smile for the camera; his head and face look larger and more mature than his small body and podgy arms.

There is also a silent film, to which Wills added a commentary some years later. Wills is put out that the film-maker devoted so much of the film to a camping expedition, but he himself had probably become too used to the huge emptiness of the hills to realise how powerfully the scenery strikes a newcomer. I visited the valley in 2000, after having read a good deal about Barns, and was astonished by the sparseness of the population. What Wills describes as the "village" of Kirkton Manor, where the boys went to buy sweets at the post office, is not more than four or five houses, one of which is the lodge at the foot of the long drive to Barns. A little way out from the village there is a junction where the signpost points up the valley to a place ten miles away, and beside it there is a "no through road" sign. The farms are spaced out along the river, and above them rise the untenanted hills. For boys from the slums of Edinburgh the sight must have been overwhelming.

Not that the boys were overwhelmed by the time they reached camp. You see them chopping wood, feeding the fire, cooking, playing games and washing up. It reminded me closely of the camps I used to organise at

Boys with guineapigs

Dartington in the 1970s, though the children I went with were ten or older, and some Barns boys were as young as eight.

Wills, in his commentary, remarks that every boy at Barns learned to swim, without instruction. There is symbolical significance in this. They also learned self-respect without instruction. Wills even remarks in *The Barns Experiment*, "If I had my way attendance at classes in such a place as Barnes would, I think, be voluntary."

Other evidence of the success of Barns is the relationship with one of the local farms. Over shots of the boys standing with a shepherd as his dog herds his flock, Wills tells the story of their first encounter with a farmer. He arrived at the door, furious that some of his gates had been left open, certainly, in his opinion, by the Barns boys. Some boys went to his farm to apologise, and were so interested by what they saw that he talked to them for some time, and invited them to come again. In the end Wills was complaining to the farmer that he was keeping them away from their studies. As well as the scene on the hillside, the film shows the boys feeding cows, and helping with the harvest. All the young men were away at the war, so any help was welcome. Mr. Barr, the one farmer still living in the valley who was there during the war, remembered boys helping with the potato harvest.

They also had a good relationship with Mrs. Anderson, at the post office and small shop in the lodge at the end of the drive. She frequently sent up boxes of sweets for the boys, using, as Wills says in the Warden's report for January 1941, "the excuse that they are cheap sweets and she does not like to sell such cheap stuff, but she does not explain why in that case she buys it, nor does that explain why one night last week she walked all the way up from Manor with two dozen bottles of mineral water for the boys."

They also got on well with the warden of a nearby youth hostel, as is shown by this passage about her from David Wills' report for September 1941.

> *When friends in Peebles attempted to commiserate with her about having the dreadful Barns boys to contend with, she replied that commiseration was unnecessary as she had come to like them very much. She said that they were very helpful, and shewed much more real courtesy than many of the superficially well-mannered boys from High Schools who sometimes came to the [Youth] Hostel in parties. She has suggested that they have a Hallowe'en party at the Hostel.*

As far as basic literacy and numeracy go, Ben Stoddard recorded in 1944 that the average increase in reading age over the last twelve months had been 1.6 years, and the average increase in arithmetic had been one year in the last six months.

At the same time Miss MacDonald was writing to the Scottish Education Department as follows:

A group on the front steps

It is one thing to bring about improvements in character, conduct and schooling and this has been done at Barns in a most gratifying way. It is another to maintain those improvements, and in that our experience has not been so happy. For this, three things are necessary:

> *(a) The boy must remain at Barns for a fairly long period after a "cure" seems to have been effected, so that the gains may be consolidated and stabilised.*
> *(b) He must not return to his home environment if this is very unsuitable.*
> *(c) Suitable employment must be found when he leaves.*

With regard to (a) our experience has been most unfortunate. Of 46 boys who have so far left, 32 left for wholly unsatisfactory or irrelevant reasons, in most cases at the behest of parents, and against advice. Three left because, in the course of treatment, they got into trouble with the police. The remaining eleven left either because we thought they were sufficiently improved to be rebilleted, or because they had reached school-leaving age. The three who left following trouble with the Police are all in Approved Schools. Of the 32 who left for unsatisfactory reasons, seven have since been sent to Approved Schools, one is in an Institute for Mental Defectives, and two have been fined for theft. All of these "failures" left against our strongly expressed advice, and five were only with us for a month or less.

Of these 32 "unsatisfactory" leavers –

> *6 stayed for a month or less*
> *4 stayed for 1 to 6 months*
> *7 stayed for 7 to 12 months*
> *5 stayed for 13 to 18 months*
> *4 stayed for 19 to 24 months*
> *4 stayed for 25 to 30 months*
> *1 stayed for 31 months*
> *1 stayed for 38 months*

The last two boys were really "ready" to leave, but we saw no point in their changing schools before they were fourteen. They were, however, removed by their parents. Seven of these boys had two periods at Barns, three of them were for various reasons refused re-admission when they applied for it.

Of the eleven who left "satisfactorily", two have since given cause for anxiety, but seem now to be getting on well.

With regard to (b) our experience has been a little happier, in the sense that we have at least been able to control the environment of the "satisfactory" leavers. Three of these were re-billeted, three were placed in farm employment in Peeblesshire, two are living in a flat provided for the purpose in Edinburgh, under suitable supervision, two returned to fairly satisfactory homes, and one was found suitable resident employment in a hotel by his father.

Our experience under (c) is again limited by the fact that so few parents left their children with us until they reached school-leaving age. Four of the "satisfactory" leavers were still at school, the remainder were all found satisfactory employment, except the one whose father found him a suitable job.

Most of this work, as well as the supervision of the Barns flat [a flat in Edinburgh where Barns boys could stay when they left], and general liaison between Barns and the boys' homes, has been carried out a by a part-time Social Worker, whom we look upon as an integral and essential part of the scheme. It is our view however, that too much stress can be laid upon the need to fit a 14 years-old boy into an ideally suitable job. At their age little is lost and much may be gained by an experimental period of a year or so. We are not unduly depressed if a boy does not settle down to the first job he gets.

The idea that anyone should be expected to find an ideally suitable job at the age of fourteen now seems extraordinarily optimistic, but at that time it was the official school-leaving age and it was not only Barns boys who found themselves on the labour market so young. However, a score of eleven successes out of forty-six does not at first sight seem impressive.

On the other hand, eleven successes with the only eleven boys who stayed until the hostel was satisfied with their recovery seems like a thorough vindication of its methods. Of the thirty-two who left, as Miss MacDonald says, "unsatisfactorily", she mentions seven sent to approved schools, one in an Institute for Mental Defectives and two fined for theft. This not only emphasises the depth of the problems faced by some of the children at Barns, but also leaves the possibility that at least some of the other twenty-two were able to fit happily into the communities they returned to.

The authenticity of these figures is confirmed by a report from Ben Stoddard, who went on to run Barns School, the residential school for maladjusted children which took the place of the hostel when it was no longer necessary as a war emergency. The boys who were accepted there had similar problems to the evacuees, and he made an analysis of what had happened to those who had left by May 1950.

45 had left since January 1945.
15 had left at the end of their school days to start work and were doing well.
14 had gone home after a short period, and were doing well.
9 had been transferred to other special schools [7 to "schools for dull and backward children" and 2 to approved schools after committing crimes in the local town.]
7 had left Barns and got into further trouble:
4 of these had been removed by parents against urgent advice.
2 had returned to very unsuitable homes.
1 had been referred by the Court to a Child Guidance Clinic.

Drawing Conclusions

The last shot in the film about Barns shows David Wills emerging from the building with a small boy sitting on his shoulders. It seems strange that Wills himself should have claimed that he had "most of the common disqualifications for dealing with young people."

> *I am reserved in manner and not easily approachable, and I find it very difficult to make contact with other people, especially with children; I find that in talking to them I am inclined to be either fatuously facetious or ponderously pompous – I can hardly ever talk to them casually and naturally. I am quick-tempered and my gorge rises far too easily for the preservation of that equanimity that is so essential. Above all (or should I say below all?) I have that worst possible of vices – I am addicted to sarcasm.*
>
> **The Barns Experiment, p. 140**

I asked Kenneth Roberton whether this could possibly be true, and he replied that yes, it was, up to a point. I mentioned the shot in the film and he said that of course the boys would clamber over David. "So he was not unapproachable at all," I said. "No, he wasn't to them," replied Roberton. "They liked him, and they respected us both in various strange ways."

Howard Jones, who worked with Wills at Bodenham Manor, wrote in 1980, "He really did listen to children, and was willing to learn from them."

Why did Wills put himself down so emphatically? Kenneth Roberton thought that it was his inner personality that he was describing, the man who had been known as Basher Wills at the Wallingford Farm Colony, who had become a Quaker and had learnt to keep his aggressive feelings under control. Craig Fees, of the PETT Archive, suggests that perhaps he was not putting himself down at all, but was merely being honest and showing a characteristic self-awareness.

I would suggest that it was also a kind of exaggerated modesty. Wills, being far too self-critical to risk any statement that might be seen as complacent, was perhaps erring in the opposite direction.

And a fourth possible explanation is that he was underplaying his personal influence in order to stress the importance of his methods. As a Quaker he looked for that of God in everyone, including the most unappealing of all the boys who came to Barns. "They must be loved," he wrote, "in order that they may learn to love. That is not only Christian teaching; it is sound modern psychology." (**The Barns Experiment, p. 79**)

He almost confessed to this in the passage immediately following his list of disqualifications for working with children.

Fortunately several of my colleagues have supplied the qualities I lack, and there is no doubt in my mind that if they had been under the leadership of a man better qualified for working with children their efforts would have met with even greater success. Provided – the proviso is of fundamental importance – provided that he had also that one virtue to which I have confessed. ... What I confess to, then, is an invincible faith in the methods we have employed and, what is more important, in the spirit which informs those methods. It is a faith that cannot be dimmed by set-backs and apparent failures, because it is based on a firmer foundation than the merely empirical; and because I know that any failures are failures in me, and not the method.

The Barns Experiment, p. 140

He "knew" this because of his faith in God, whose will he was seeking to obey. He felt that it was difficult for anyone to carry on a regime like that at Barns or in Homer Lane's Little Commonwealth unless their methods had a spiritual origin. He played down his own contribution because he was only working as best he could towards objectives ordained by God.

One of the women staff at Barns who had been suffering from continual abuse from a particular boy came to Wills one day and asked how she could possibly continue to love him. Wills' reply was that she must feign love; whenever she saw him approaching she must imagine him to be one of the boys she liked best, and treat him exactly as if he was that boy. He claims that he made up the reply spontaneously, and was surprised when she came back to him later and told him how well the idea had worked – she had been able to treat the boy with apparent affection, and he had responded with real affection for her and now there was a genuine bond between them.

I don't think Wills ever had to feign love himself. He not only understood the necessity for it from a theoretical point of view, he actually responded personally to the boys' desperate need. This meant that he was accused of doing something unique and inimitable – and this was intended as a criticism, not praise. He was accused of failing to demonstrate a system that could be used by others for the benefit of other children, but doing something that came naturally to him, and that only he could do.

If his system was to be imitated, he had to defend himself against this accusation. He had to try to establish that it was not because of his personal qualities that Barns succeeded, but because of the principles upon which it was run. No-one else could be David Wills, but anyone who shared his principles could do what he had done.

When he was due to leave the hostel in 1945, the Birmingham Society for the Care of Invalid and Nervous Children planned to employ him to start a new school. The Special Services Branch of the Ministry of Education was dubious about this proposal, and sent a Mr. Arbuckle, from the Scottish Education Department, to find out what he could about him. Here are some extracts from an official account of Mr. Arbuckle's report – the negative report I mentioned earlier. He seems to have set out to find things that he thought were wrong, and in doing so he has caricatured himself as a blind adherent to convention who cannot bear even to consider any alternative.

In addition to receiving information from various sources Mr. Arbuckle visited the hostel once and thus gained first-hand impressions of Mr. Wills. The latter believed in very free discipline which in some respects did not conform to ordinary social standards, e.g. the children need not wash their hands before meals if they did not wish to do so, no form of punishment was meted out for misdeeds and an undue familiarity between him and them was permitted. He was somewhat self-opinionated in that he did not consider that he had anything to learn from persons engaged in similar work.

Mr. Arbuckle sensed a feeling of suspicion and mistrust about Mr. Wills and his methods and thought he was being untrue to himself. He did not think Mr. Wills was actually dishonest judging from his own peculiar standards but there was something indefinitely wrong which suggested that Mr. Wills was not suitable for dealing with children. Opinions varied about him from suggesting that he did produce some fruitful results with a few of the children to that of asserting that he was a hypocrite. Mr. Arbuckle favoured one mid-way between these two, but he definitely considered that employment of Mr. Wills should be approved only with the greatest caution.

The wealth of misunderstandings in this encounter would be hilarious if it had not had such serious consequences. Wills was appointed, but the Ministry remained hostile. The school never received unqualified official support, and after eleven years of frustration, disagreement and disappointment, Wills resigned.

In spite of the way some of the least promising young citizens of Edinburgh had developed and matured under his care at Barns, his work was seldom imitated and was soon forgotten by those outside his immediate field[2]. Even many of those working in the same field preferred to continue in their Arbuckle ways, however unsuccessful they might be, rather than to try out

2   The phrase "soon forgotten" has been contradicted by Craig Fees. He points out , for instance, that Wills was awarded the OBE, that a new residential building has been named after him at Glebe Therapeutic Community in Cambridgeshire and that there is an annual lecture in his honour, instigated in his lifetime by the Association of Workers for Maladjusted Children. The 2001 lecture, by John Visser of Birmingham University, centred very much on David Wills, and was given again at the association's annual conference.

anything like the Barns system. Either they stuck to the excuse that only David Wills himself could do it, or they simply refused to accept "a very free discipline which in some respects did not conform to ordinary social standards," and nothing David Wills himself could say would make them change their minds.

Doctor Pedro Albizu Campos Puerto Rican High School

History

The Doctor Pedro Albizu Campos Puerto Rican High School in Chicago started in 1972. It was not founded by adults with a clear educational philosophy but by a group of eight students, led by Norma I. Reyes, who had all been expelled from the local high school for fomenting a student strike.

The strike had been in protest against the sacking of two teachers who had been teaching Puerto Rican history and culture, and speaking Spanish in the classroom. The fact that these were sacking offences needs some explanation.

The first Puerto Ricans in the United States were not willing immigrants. Puerto Rico was simply taken over by the American military in 1898, and martial law was imposed for the first two years of the occupation. The United States then introduced an economic plan that strangled the economy to such an extent that many people had to emigrate to the US in the hope of a better future. When they arrived they found themselves forced into ghettoes in New York and Chicago, where they worked in dead-end jobs for minimal wages.

Puerto Rico has never become part of the USA; it remains a colony, and there is a strong independence movement both on the island and within the United States. Teaching Puerto Ricans about their history and culture was therefore deemed by the government to be a subversive activity. The Puerto Ricans in Chicago had not merely been denied a national identity, they had also been driven away from the desirable sites on the lake front, where urban renewal had driven up prices, and had collected mainly into the area around Humboldt Park, in the north-west part of Chicago. This had at first seemed a good idea to the dominant white community, because it kept the Puerto Ricans out of the rest of the city. However, being all in one area and sharing a common language, the Puerto Ricans were able to organise themselves; representatives of the first generation to have been brought up in Chicago began to go to college, to start clinics and childcare facilities and to look after themselves in ways that the civil authorities had ignored.

Almost all the staff at Tuley, the local High School, were suburban whites who had a patronising attitude to the youth of the area, most of whom they regarded as criminally inclined and barely educable. The director of the present-day Puerto Rican Cultural Centre, José Lopez, was educated at Tuley and for a time went back there to teach. He tells a story to illustrate the

Murals of Puerto Rican political prisoners outside the Cultural Centre

attitude of the white staff. One of their number was asleep in the staff room; another put a notice near him saying, "Quiet please. Puerto Ricans at work."

The white teachers at Tuley saw it as their duty to teach the Puerto Rican students to become good Americans. There were therefore three reasons why Spanish could not be allowed in the school: firstly, because the teachers wouldn't be able to understand what was being said and therefore would not be able to keep order; secondly, because if their students were to become good Americans they would have to speak English; and thirdly because a secret language would give the students the opportunity to plan against the state.

For those of us who see the advantages of being able to speak more than one language this attitude seems, to say the least, narrow-minded, but at that time it was forbidden to use any language other than English in a Chicago classroom.

The two teachers who went as far as actually teaching in Spanish were immensely popular with the students, but when the authorities found out what was going on they were first suspended and then sacked. Three hundred of the two thousand students walked out immediately in solidarity with them. They formulated demands which they presented to the school, the local community joined in demonstrations and eventually the whole school was closed down for a week. The reaction of the administration was to call in the police, who have a particular reputation for brutality in Chicago. The police attacked the demonstrators, the demonstrators fought back and there were full-scale riots.

When the riots were over, the demonstrators' demands had still not been met, but the eight students who were expelled as the leaders of the strike started their own school. They were supported by Carmen Valentin, who was one of the teachers who had been sacked, and such people as Rev. José Torres and Oscar Lopez Rivera, members of the local community. These people gave classes in Puerto Rican history and culture, as well as the Spanish language, in the basement of a church on Agusta Avenue.

The rights to teach Puerto Rican history and culture and to speak Spanish in the classroom, important as they are, do not seem a likely foundation for a whole new educational approach, but the fact that the High School had been started by students was extremely important, and it soon differentiated itself sharply from the conventional schools in the neighbourhood in other ways as well.

Puerto Rico has never been without a coloniser, so the school system has never been under the control of Puerto Ricans, even on the island itself. US history books barely mention Puerto Rico at all, except to say when it was taken over. The students and teachers in the new school were inspired by the idea of studying their nation's history, but they found that there were no textbooks in English or Spanish, so they had to do their own research. This led on to the study of all things Puerto Rican, including the music, the dancing and the food.

Many of the first students, and others who came after them, had drug problems, family problems or gang problems, and sometimes all three. Leading figures from the locality came in to address health questions, to talk about the way they were trying to create a community, to give the students back their self-respect. This entailed a process of self-discovery for the teachers as well as the students.

For the first four years the school remained very small, and the curriculum was guided by the wishes of the students. They went on demonstrations against abuses of human rights, and became active members of the Puerto Rican community. The teachers found that they had become facilitators and organisers rather than authority figures.

In 1976 the school moved to the premises it occupied until the time I was there (2001). The number of students was increasing so more staff had to be taken on. A dialogue began with other alternative schools; most of them were rural and predominantly white, but they had many of the same aims, including, most importantly, the idea that the students should be in control of their own education. The difference was that at the Puerto Rican High School the students shared their control with the community, the teachers and the activists who were trying to change the nature of the living conditions for the people in the Chicago West Side.

I spent a week there in November 1999, and heard about the racism, the gangs and the social background of the students at first hand.[1]

Racism and Gangs

Ada Rivera was a self-possessed, elegant young woman who you might at first sight guess to be twenty-two or twenty-three and well on her way in some successful career. In fact she was seventeen, and working to graduate from High School. She had started at Albizu Campos a year before my visit, and I asked her why she had come.

---

1   Most of the quotations in the following text are taken from recorded interviews, though a few come from letters or emails. I have changed the order of some of the responses, and some hesitations and repetitions have been edited out. Double negatives, which are correct in Spanish but sound strange in standard English, have usually been retained.

I was having trouble in public school. I was attending a vocational school. I was there for two years, and for the two years I was there I didn't do anything. If you were to talk to any of my teachers, that knew the work that I could hand in, they would tell you, "She's a good student, she's very fine, she just hasn't applied herself," they would say – or that I really wasn't, you know, paying attention.

The first year, it was true, I wasn't paying attention, but by the second year I was already more focussed and ready to learn, and my teachers just gave up on me. And I'm the type of student that sits in the back of the classroom, and if you don't keep me attentive, then I'm not going to pay attention, I'm just going to go to sleep. Because what you're saying to me doesn't make sense to me and I don't care. And I had that uncare attitude for a while and then when I started to come to my teachers and telling them, "Look, I could do this, you know that, this work is not really any problem for me, I just need help because I'm falling behind," they told me that I should just drop out of school.

When I was in third grade there was a girl who spoke Spanish only, she didn't speak any English, and I told them, and I used to explain the lessons to her in Spanish so that she could do the work. She started to tell me, "I'm going to get in trouble because I don't do the work," so I just said, "Look, I'll explain it to you in Spanish, so we've got to talk a little." Whenever the teacher would explain what's going on, I would explain it to her in Spanish. Well, one day the teacher heard me, and she hit me with a ruler. She told me that I was in America, that I should speak English, and I should forget about Spanish because I'm not in Puerto Rico and that's not my language. I should speak English, because I'm in America, and I'm American. I told her I'm Puerto Rican, and she was like, "Not any more." And other times I've had teachers tell me, "You're just a Puerto Rican, you're not going to amount to anything, you're not going to make as much money as me."

I asked her whether she had met much racism.

Yes. In Miami I was affected by racism, but not just from whites. It was black and white people. I guess from all the racism with whites and Latinos and blacks – all the racism somehow just meshed to the point where everybody was segregated. And in Miami that's how it is, everybody is just segregated, the whites live with the whites, the Latinos with the Latinos, the blacks with the blacks. The Latinos are basically like – Puerto Ricans and Cubans. A lot of people migrate from Cuba and from Haiti, and they go to Miami, and there's a lot of segregation, people stick to their own kind, they're on that level.

When I got here to Chicago, racism really didn't affect me until I started to get older, and I started to go places, where I began to realise that I was the different one. You see I'm the first one to be graduating from high school from my family, on time, and I'm going to be the first one that's going to go on to college right away after high school. My Mom finished high school when she was thirty years old. She got her diploma and she's taking college courses and all that but I'm going to be the first one to just go and do it.

A lot of times I find myself in the position where I go somewhere and because of the colour of my skin or because of the way I look, people perceive things of me. They get these bad perceptions of me, because they see this Latina girl who is coming from Humboldt Park, she's ghetto, she's bad. We're moving house and even just yesterday I met a landlord and he looked at me, and the first thing he thought – he even told me – the first thing that came into his mind was that he thought I was a troublemaker. Because I have the look on my face.

I know I may look like a troublemaker sometimes. I don't act like a normal seventeen-year-old girl acts. I'm smarter. I'm smart, I'm direct, I'm to the point, I don't beat around the bush. A lot of people take that the wrong way, they look at me and they think, "Oh-oh, she's a trouble-maker," or, "That's the bad one." And I'm not, you know, I'm the quiet one. I don't speak until I have something to say but when I say, I speak my mind.

I've been affected by racism, especially with police. Police pull us over in our neighbourhood, and I've had male cops try to search me because they think I'm stupid and I don't know my rights. And when I tell them, "Look, I know my rights, you can't even do this to me," they threaten to hit me. I've had cops purposely mess with me because I was wearing a shirt that has all the Puerto Rican political prisoners on the back. We were all standing outside, and the cop came and pulled us over. The guys were all on their knees. They told all the guys to kneel down and put their hands on their heads and all the girls were standing up, and when they saw my shirt they were like, "All of youse too, get down too!" And all the girls had to go on their knees too, and they started reading my shirt and they started like messing with me, and they were like, "So when are you going to add your name to the back of the shirt?" I've lived through a lot of drama with police and racism, and even with my teachers. My teachers just used to tell me, "Well, you're Puerto Rican, why don't you just stay at home and make babies."

The High School was planning to move to a new site on Division Street. This was in order to come closer to the heart of the Puerto Rican community, and to escape from the gentrification that was beginning to fill the area with yuppies. The new site was not far away, but I had heard that some of the students would not be able to attend the school when it moved, and a young man with baggy jeans, a sweater, a big coat and a hat even indoors, explained this to me.

The reason why some of the students won't be able to go over there is because of gangs, violence and all. Misunderstanding between the gangs. Most of us, like myself, we used to be in gangs, and now that we're out of that they still know us out there. Especially on Division, there's a lot of people that recognise our faces, so it would be a danger to us, and also to the other students of the school if we kept on going to the school when they move over there.[2]

There's the Dragons, the Jivers, the Almighty Imperial Gangster Nation, the Maniac Disciples, the Gangster Disciples, the Milwaukee Kings and the Spanish Cobras.

I used to be an I.G. [Imperial Gangster] and I used to gangbang and I've been shot, stabbed.

I had to ask for an explanation of the word "gangbang".

Me, I used to be a gangbanger. That means I'd be out on the street hustling, making my money, making sure that no other gangs come to my neighbourhood trying to kill one of ours. A gangster's mentality is, "You kill one of mine, I gotta kill two of yours." They think that it's respect. "They gotta respect my block." That ain't their block. I mean nobody owns it. They don't own it. It's not like the block is named after them. It's things like that that I've realised, that I've seen, that made me think this way. And that's the meaning of gangbang.

I've seen my family, most of my family, die. All around me my best friends getting killed. Just this week, on Wednesday, my cousin, eleven years old, he just got killed, and all through this, over little misunderstandings and everything. And even just because of the gang colours that people don't know that they're wearing. They get shot over stupid things.

And mainly what I don't understand is all that violence is going on while the heads of every single gang is always smoking with each other, with all the heads, they're always having sessions and making business with each other, while youngsters are out there killing each other and everything.

The gangs fight for neighbourhoods, for the block that they want, or over drug territory, drug trafficking, things like that. They mainly fight with each other. If somebody kills one of theirs, they think out of respect they got to go and kill two of theirs. They operate mainly like that.

What we call to go out and kill each other, we call that peeling caps. The way they do that is they do it organised. Like, I remember, they were planning

2   Lourdes Lugo, who became head of the school in 2001, recently sent me this comment: "Since the interviews many things have changed on Division Street, including that many of the students that will be moving with us feel much more safe and comfortable than ever before. The development on Division Street has neutralized many of the gangs that functioned in the area, and even residents feel much more safe and secure. Although the overall situation for gangs in the city has not changed I think that the work that the Puerto Rican Cultural Centre has done in the last three years has paved the way to a more secure site."

on killing somebody called Big Julie. He was a Nieta out in Hartford, Connecticut, he was very, very dangerous. He killed my cousin's girlfriend, he killed so many people that were Solidos and Solidas, so we made what we call a junta. That means we all get together, we make a decision on what is going to happen to a person that is a danger to us.

Mainly out there, what I like about the Solidos was we worried about going out killing everybody, we were more organised, we cared more about the community of Puerto Ricans than what the gangs out here do. It's like the Latin Kings in New York, they're organised, they're not about gangbanging and killing each other and what not. Their object is to help the community, that's their first priority. That was our first priority in Hartford, Connecticut. So that's one thing I like about it.

When you peel a cap you always have to have double clothes, double jeans, double shirt if you go and kill somebody. So they won't identify you you change your clothes. Quick. So that you have the clothes, you change them.

The old ones is what we call the OGs, they call them original gangsters. In a gang once you pass the limit of twenty-one you become one of the bigheads, you become like wiser, you're no more use to them because you're already old. To them you're old, you know, you can't be a soldier no more. Mainly the soldiers are all young people, I mean eleven, ten, twelve, thirteen, real young kids that are out there killing each other over a street that doesn't even belong to them. They're fighting over things that they don't even know what they're really fighting for. They don't know the meaning of the fight that they do, you know, the struggles that are happening to them. It's bad, because I see all these shorties dying over things that they don't even know about.

They got guns. They kill. As we speak, they're out there, keeping security, what we call that, they'll be in each corner making sure that nobody gets through unknown, or something. If another gang tries to creep up on them or that's how we say down here, like somebody tries to come and do something to them, they already see them, and they already know it. These kids are eleven, twelve years old with guns, killing each other, not knowing better, you know.

...

It's very hard to get out once you're in. I mean, for me, like, I was one of the big heads in Hartford, Connecticut. I was also in a gang out there called the True Solid Organization, and I got out easy because I'm one of the heads, so I got out, they let me walk right out. Mainly for other people, you gotta get a beatdown. Sometimes they even kill you while you're trying to get out. They send you to the hospital. They break your ribs. In order to get down, to get out, you've got to receive a beatdown – violation, how they call it out here. It mainly is like fifty on each side and you walk straight through the middle, and while you're getting hit, you can't do nothing about it.

Me, they let me get out. I got blessed out, and right now I talk to the heads out there and I'm trying to break it up, because I don't want to see nobody else go through the things I went through at eight, nine. I was practically homeless, didn't have a place to stay, I was out on the street, my Mom kicked me out. It was very hard for me growing up. My father wasn't there because he was out here in Chicago and I was in Hartford, so it was very hard for me to do all these things, to live my life the way that I wanted to, to live my childhood the way that I wanted to. I always had to worry about my little brother, if he's going to eat. I hardly didn't eat because I always had – I always fed him before me. I was practically a father to my little brother, 'cause my Mom, she was never around, she was always out drinking, or drugs, or dancing – all these things, while my little brother was at home, starving. I had to take care of him. But it was mainly easier for me than for most of the people out here. They got to receive a beatdown and everything, you know. It's very hard for most of these youngsters.

If I catch my little brother in a gang I swear I'll – I mean I might have to probably hit him a couple of times or what not, but I'm going to show him what gangs really do, and instead of them sending them out there to kill each other they got to educate them. They got to tell them that school is the first thing, where they first should be at, that they got to finish school first, to help themself and to help other people, instead of killing each other.[3]

Chicago is divided between the Folks and the People. The Folks and the People are divided into multiple smaller gangs. If you belong to one gang, you are automatically outlawed from the territory of another. Girls who join gangs sometimes have to submit to rape; this may be multiple rape, and it may be repeated. I asked Jesse Mumm, a staff member at the school, whether it was necessary to join a gang for self-protection.

To some it is, because of where they live, and who they know. To some, it becomes impossible not to be associated with a certain gang because of their family or close friends. I cannot impress upon you enough what happens when a young man, especially, turns fourteen around here. Suddenly it seems to him that everybody wants to kick his ass or recruit him. It's a powerful incentive. But many get involved simply because it's money. It's economics. It's the local corporation that's hiring, if you're poor and desperate. It just happens to be illegal.

You can refuse to join, and half the time nothing happens to you. But if a gang is "sweating" you to join, you will have to get beat up, usually more than once, to prove you are not going to change your mind.

---

3   Two years after my interview with this young man, he was back on the streets of Hartford. He had to raise the money to support the children he had fathered. Even a school like the Doctor Pedro Albizu Campos High School cannot solve every problem.

The vast majority of young people are not in gangs. I can't emphasize that enough. But eventually all are somehow seen as gang members by the people in authority: teachers, cops, the government, the media.

We have several young women who are active members. Not all gangs require the literal ritual gangbang, but many do. And for some, it is an ongoing requirement. Every gang has its women's section – the Latin Kings have the Queens, the Disciples have the D-Lettes, and on and on. I would guess they are in it with the men at about a 2:1 ratio.

Marvin Garcia, the principal of the school, described the situation like this.

We do have gang members in the school, but I don't recognise them as gang members. I recognise them as the individuals that they are. It's one individual, not one of the Team, or the Latin Eagles, or the Folks, or the People. I know as soon as they leave the school they're doing their thing, but this is the big challenge before us.

The gangs offer a lot more, sometimes, than what we can offer. They offer four or five hundred dollars a night – more than that – you know, selling drugs, or moving drugs from one place to another. I remember a young woman, who told me that she was running money for cocaine from the stock exchange in to the drug dealers. All these people, all these rich people getting high, and what she was doing was bringing the money to the drug dealers, and she was making good money doing that. Who can compete with that? There she is, fifteen years old, she had nice clothes, she had nice gym shoes, a nice jacket, and all she was doing was running the money. That's it. She was really open about it.

The gangbangers sell drugs, but they're also in competition; they start up with other gangs, and the other gangs want to pitch it out. They don't want to rub you out, they want the market. So when one gang writes on the wall, "This is our area," it means it's their turf, it's their market. It's like the war, like World War II, yeah? The market. The marketplace. So if one gang has a wall for selling drugs and things, if another gang comes and throws their colours on it, that means they're saying, "We're going to fight you for this market. We're going to take this market from you." That's what it is.

A youth says, "Here, go shoot this person. Here's a gun. Here, you do this, because you're a kid, so if you're arrested you don't have to do that much time."

And of course you have the issue of police in the community who constantly don't know how to work with them. They keep them in gangs and drive them to gangs, just beat 'em up and call them names. They pick them up in one section and drop them off in the middle of their rival gang and say, "Good luck," or, "Here, come and get 'em."

The police do not know how to work with the gangs. They make an attempt, but they're looking down at the young people as though there's something wrong with them, rather than saying there's something wrong with the structure of the society. They're looking at them as criminals and looking at them as predators, and they don't have no problem with laws that incarcerate you at a younger age, or laws that say you can't be on a street corner without getting picked up and arrested. None of those things promote you to trust so-called authority figures. They have power and authority as we know, but there's nothing there to build links, to say, "Hey, we care about you. You're going the wrong way, it's going to hurt you and in the long run it's going to hurt the community. It's hurting people. What is it that you need? Let's try to fix this."

The gang provides a lot of things. It provides money, it provides a girlfriend, it provides family, it provides parties, it provides reasons to exist. Unfortunately it won't work.

There are young people that I have worked with that have come out of the gangs, but there's a price. The price is that when you're in, you're always in, even if you're out. And if you're out, then you have more enemies – you have your former gang, and everybody else. It's hard. I'm dealing with someone in that situation right now. There are people that do work at that level, that go to gang leaders and say, "Let 'em be, you know, let 'em alone." And many of them do. Many of them do say, "OK, we're calling off this – search and destroy mission on this person." They don't call them like that, they call them like SOS, Smash On Sight, or KOS, which is the worst one, Kill On Sight.

The gangs used to just defend their – let's say their communities. There was the Polish gang, or the Puerto Rican gang, or the Latino gang. Now all the gangs have become multinational. It's not about defending the community any more, it's about selling the drugs and making the money.

Inside the school

During the week I was there I found the school friendly, informal and full of laughter. When the students arrive in the morning, greetings include hugs and kisses for staff as well as fellow students. Discussions tend to be noisy, because everyone has an opinion and they all want to make their opinions heard. Participation is encouraged. No matter what it is like in the streets outside, inside the school everyone gets along. As another student, Andreina Colon, told me:

The new guys come in and they act like they're hardcore. I guess because they don't know what to expect and after a while from being here you get to know them real well, and you find out the real them – most of them are goofy, some are shy, there's all kinds of people here.

The students I interviewed were so open and genuine that I felt a real affection for them, as if I had known them for a long time. Something makes these hardcore new guys change, and some do so very quickly.

When my cousin – may he rest in peace, he's fifteen, just turned sixteen – he died last year, at the beginning of last year – that really changed me, because he died in my arms. This year in August, my other cousin, may he rest in peace, he was thirteen, he died right in front of me, too. It's like things that – I brought them into the gangs, and everything, and now, you know, I have this burden, I feel like it was my responsibility once I got out to get them out, and I couldn't do that, I couldn't save their life. You know, so it's very hard.

I changed all my ways. Well, I probably drink once in a while but not like I used to, I don't gangbang no more, I don't hang out any more. I'm mainly concentrated on my school work, concentrating on my life now, changing, trying to change myself for the better. Even though I still got the mentality that what I did to somebody is going to come back to me, to haunt me and everything, so that every day I just live my life, day by day, you know, looking forward to the next day. That's how I live my life.

Marvin described the school's approach to the gang problem.

There's one thing that we have going for us, and that's the ethical struggle. We say, "Look, maybe there isn't an option, but let's understand that when you're doing this you're bringing down the community, poisoning the community. You're destroying life. You're doing the opposite of what we're trying to do. We're trying to uplift the community. We're trying to help people to take control of their lives, and live their lives with dignity, and what you're doing is objectifying our community, enslaving our community. It's a reality that it's very hard to get out of. We can't compete. We'll help you, we'll help you go to college, we'll help you, but it's very difficult."

Esmeralda Arceo, who was sixteen, had been at the school for two years, and had a wonderfully patient baby called Carlos, who occasionally interrupted our interview by trying to put the microphone in his mouth. She had chosen to come to Albizu Campos for reasons that were nothing to do with gangs.

I wanted a small place, I wanted a place where the teachers would listen to me, help me out more with my work, and I guess I was captured by the family atmosphere.

My first year of high school was actually in a public high school, and I really didn't like it. It was like teachers who weren't interested in showing us more than there was when they lectured us, opened the book and told us, "You have to do this and that," and, "Any questions?" They really didn't care.

Although I did well in studies, I was always a nerd. I like learning and all of that. I didn't feel that a public school was the right place for me because, even though I didn't look for problems, I always had people like picking on me,

Esmeralda Arceo and Carlos

and I said, "If I stay in a public school I'm going to end up dropping out and getting into a fight and everything. I don't want that."

Here people are really talkative. If they see you, that you're not talking, they go up to you and they talk to you. And the teachers are the same way, they always try to get the students to talk to each other, and build their friendship, relationship.

I asked whether having a baby had made a difference.

Actually it did, because if I had been in a regular high school I would have had to stop going to school as soon as my stomach started showing and when I got pregnant here I always had a welcome from the teachers as well as the students. And they have this program downstairs that is called the Family Learning Centre, and they take care of the baby while I'm at school. I only go downstairs to change his diaper and I feed him during lunch. So it's really good.

I'm graduating this year, and I'm intending going on to college. Have to see how that works with the baby. And after that I want to be a doctor, so I'll have to manage time for the baby and study and all of that.

Here I usually stay after school with the baby so I can do my work, because it's really hard at home. So I've managed to stay after school like until four, four thirty. I do my work, I ask the teachers to help me, and that's how I do it, because if I go to my house after school I won't get anything done. My mother used to help me out a lot, but I'm not living with my mother right now, I'm living with the baby's father. He's working right now. He's getting paid like seven an hour. It's been really good with his job. I'm not working.

Esmeralda mentioned "this program downstairs that is called the Family Learning Centre". The high school, which had around seventy students, was housed in the same warehouse building as the Puerto Rican Cultural Centre, which ran a variety of programs on the ground floor. The high school used the basement as a canteen and a few rooms on the ground floor, but spent most of its time on the first floor, in what used to be the offices. There was a long, carpeted, central space with two tables where three or four people could work, one long multi-seater sofa and one very short one. The classrooms ran along the sides of this hallway. The hallway was lined with noticeboards, and hung with banners listing the names of graduates, and a Puerto Rican flag.

The outside of the building was decorated with portraits of some of the fifteen Puerto Rican political prisoners who had been in prison until only a year or two previously. Each portrait filled the equivalent of a window bay. The street was attractively wide and planted with young trees, but close at hand were building sites where old factories and houses had been knocked down and were being replaced by blocks of expensive apartments. The process of gentrification was removing opportunities for work at the same time as it priced the local population out of the housing market.

There was only one entrance to the school and the cultural centre, and at the office there they checked everyone who went in or out. Students had to stay inside the school on the upper floor until they could all move down to the basement for lunch together, or leave together at the end of the school day. The staff stood outside the school with the students until they had all gone. It looked like a friendly social occasion, but it was more than that. It was also to keep away drug-dealers and gang members, and to protect the students from actual violence. The staff are a protection because they represent the Puerto Rican Community Centre, for which even the gangbangers show a surprising amount of respect. Nevertheless, only a few days after I left a red sedan drove past the group on the pavement and flashed a gun at a student who was living under a KOS order. A teacher patrolled round the block to make sure the car had gone.

The leaflet which advertises the school gives a list of the advantages it has to offer. At the top of the list is "Safe Environment". When I first saw it I did not understand why this should come before such things as "Small class size" and "Individual attention", and there was nothing in the atmosphere inside the school to explain it. The environment did indeed seem welcoming and secure, but so what? It was only when I began to hear a little about what happened in the streets outside, and about students' previous experiences in the regular high schools, that I realised that the safety of the environment was not only vitally important, but also something of a miracle.

Carlos Rodriguez, a twenty-year-old student, told me this:

Where I live they do a lot of drugs and they do a lot of violence, and I've got to watch my back every time. I always watch. I don't trust nobody. The only one I trust is God. He's the only one I trust. It is dangerous, where I live, it is dangerous. It's really dangerous. Too much gang members, too much drugs. I'm like I'm tired of . . . I got to live with that, and they don't mess with me. They don't. So – that's no worry.

I was born in Puerto Rico. I was there for sixteen years and a half. I didn't like it, but my grandma raised me for sixteen years. I came here, I went to a school, I didn't know no English, I didn't do nothing. For two weeks I was out of school, and then my aunt found out about this school. I've been here since '95. I like the school, and I'm proud about it, and I don't care what anybody say, they say, "Oh, look, you're twenty, you're supposed to be out of high school." You know what? I don't care. I'm going to get my diploma. And I don't care what anybody say.

In the classroom

Michael Flores, a sixteen-year-old who had been in the school for six months, told me it was the best school in Chicago. I asked him why he had left his last school.

There was too many gangs. Too many violence. Me, I got jumped twice. That's why my mother took me out of that school, because she doesn't want to see me die.

I asked him to explain the phrase, "I got jumped."

It means I got beat up in that school. Like two-three times. And the teachers and the principals, they didn't do nothing because they can't do nothing about it. So I got out of it.

I heard about this school because my friend goes here. I got here, I was made to take a test, that was OK, and I got in. The students all get along. You'll see no fights up here. They don't want to fight. That's the good thing about this school. If you go to Kelvin you'll see a lot of fights and stuff. Or Clemente. Or any other school like that – public schools. Here I think there are some gang members, but they don't show it, though. Although they're used to all that stuff outside, they come here and they all get along. None of that gang stuff in this school.

Andreina Colon told me why she had come to the school and went on to talk about another aspect of the school that helps to build up the students' self-respect.

My brother used to come to this school. And he always felt good about it, oh, it was fun, and this and that, and when I graduated I wanted to go to Clemente, I wanted to be with my friends, but there were a lot of girls over there that I didn't like, and I knew I was going to have trouble and all that, so I decided to come here.

And I like this school, yeah.

I like how they teach here because if you don't understand something you can ask a question and the teacher will explain it to you. She'll answer my question, we'll talk about it or discuss it, it's not like in other schools, you know, so many kids the teacher just has to get on with her lesson. I like it. I like all the teachers.

It's not important that it's a Puerto Rican school, but I like the fact that it is because I'm Puerto Rican and it teaches me more about my culture and things that are going on in Puerto Rico, that you don't usually hear in the news and things like that. But I'm not just Puerto Rican, I'm Ecuadorian, too.

We learn about different places, not just Puerto Rico, because it's called a Puerto Rican high school. We learn about Mexico, we learn about a lot of Latino places. I mean we also learn about literature of the United States and history and all that. But usually in other schools you focus more on the United States, they don't go so much for Latino, South America, Central America, and here they do.

Ada Rivera put it like this:

It gave me a chance to study my own roots, my background, my own history, instead of American history. It was different because when I got here we had classes like Latino literature, Puerto Rican history, Mexican history and it was really interesting. It just caught my attention right away and I thought, "That's what I want to take," and I completely just gave all my dedication and started finding out who I was and where I came from. It was really really important for me to have that chance, because in a way it helped me to discover who I was as a person.

Outside the school

Esmeralda, who is Mexican, told how the school builds on the students' personal pride in nationhood to show them how to, as Marvin said, "move from the language of critique to the language of possibilities."

When I was taught Puerto Rican history, they didn't only teach me the history of Puerto Rico as, you know, the Spanish invasion, and all of that, they also taught me about the struggles that are happening in our day. And it's really unfair, what the US government is doing, colonising Puerto Rico, and it really interested me that the school is actually doing something about that, the Puerto Rican political prisoners and all of that. I was interested in the marches for the Puerto Rican prisoners, and the teachers always tell us, "If you're not interested in it, you don't have to go." It's just if you want to go that you can. They don't pressure us into going if we don't want to. I was interested, I've been to a lot of marches. I went to New York, that was last year, and it was about the political prisoners too, and I've been to Washington too, for the political prisoners, and now that they're out, we feel that we have accomplished our goal.

Marvin expressed the educational ideas behind this approach.

I think what's important is that our educational philosophy is not only that young people learn and ask questions, and learning and asking questions is good, but we also feel that it's part of the process of transforming the reality. We take positions in our school, it's not just you say, "OK, now we got this position settled, so we agree on this." No, it's about also taking action around it and so therefore we participate in a lot of things.

We participate in demonstrations in support of funding for the youth, particularly youth that have been pushed out of schools, funding for alternative education. Students have participated in rallies against police brutality, and creating programs to raise awareness around HIV and AIDS in our community, as well as STDs.

So, around the issue of Puerto Rico, same thing. We have been engaged for many years – it seems like almost all the years I've been director of the school. We've always discussed the issue of the political prisoners, and students have written to them, students have visited them. They have written Christmas cards to them and named things after them, and we've gone to many demonstrations that support their release. Students have gone to the Congress and lobbied and done advocacy for their release, meeting with congressional leaders, so they've been in all these processes. They've gone to the United Nations. The students have been exposed to a lot of things, and they have become agents of change.

Now eleven of the fifteen prisoners have been released, and there's a lot of students that have come in the eighties, like '85, '86, '87, they have come back to the school and said, "Wow, they're out! They're out! And I was part of that process of getting them out." Everything they did was so necessary, from the demonstrations to passing out literature in the street where people were telling them, "Get away from me," spitting on them. All of that was so hard. It was a process that we knew that was right, and we got vindication. They're out. There's still more to get out, but everybody's happy that they took part in that process of freeing the prisoners.

Now, I've been told, "That's politics, that's politics, students involved in politics." Well, education's not neutral. The public school system is teaching young people not to engage, and not to be a political force for themselves and for their communities. You need to understand and participate in the process, and sometimes – and many times – just going to the ballot box and putting down a vote isn't enough. You have to be participatory and active in that quest for social change.

This activity is not confined to demonstrations and lobbying. The Cultural Centre is connected with a project called Vida SIDA, which works for the awareness and prevention of HIV and STD. Some of the students take part in dramatic presentations as a part of this campaign. Juana Maciel, who was fifteen, is one of them.

It was funny, because I was supposed to be married to this one guy that was cheating on me with another man, and in another part I had to be a drug addict, and I had a son, a baby, and the DCSS took the baby from me because I couldn't take care of it and I was too into the drugs, and I was going crazy, I was in the nuthouse, and then afterwards I got better and they gave me my kid back and I was going to have another kid.

By where I live there really was this one lady that had a little girl – she was into alcohol and drugs and her little girl was about to get raped by another man, an older man, and the police came and took the little girl from her. And now, the years passed and she is like too much into alcohol and drugs and she passed away – last year. The little girl was like five or six.

I like to support good causes. Freedom for people, like I don't believe that one person should have control over something that is not even theirs. It makes no sense. I think everybody should be absolutely free.

Ada Rivera was a member of a group called Theatre of the Oppressed, which re-enacts things that happen in the community.

I love going to the marches, and whatever's going on. Positive things like that I support. I don't support things that's never going to help our community. We're on the come-up, we're trying to get up, you know. For a lot of years now our community's been like dragged through the mud, we've been stereotyped. There's been people who are racist against us, we've been attacked, we've been everything.

Right now our community is on the come-up, we're trying to develop our community into something bigger, something that's actually going to stay here and we're trying to say, "OK, we're not going to get pushed around." We're not going to let people come and take our community, this is our community, we're the ones that live here, we're the ones that are working on it, this is something that belongs to us." So I participate in all those things because it's positive, it's just a lot of support for the community.

I also work a lot with the Public Allies, and stuff like that. Actually we had a business program with students from the school and Public Allies. They told us the basics of owning and running your own business and we did a preliminary business plan. That was just our first couple of steps of the business and right now the business class is still going. It was a place mat business, where the students were designing place mats, and we're going to sell them to the restaurants on Division Street.

The teachers and the students

The quotations above illustrate two of the high school's tools for transforming the lives of the students: justifying pride in their nation, and encouraging active participation in political and community events. Another important aspect of the school's approach is that the students' own personal difficulties are acknowledged and the staff do all they can to help. There are, for instance, a number of counsellors who work there, and one of the displays on the noticeboards around the central hall gives advice on what to do if you get raped. I asked Andreina what were the differences between Albizu Campos and her previous school, and this was her reply:

I guess the way the teachers approach you. If you get in trouble, how they talk about it. It's the communications between students and teachers – and between students and students.

The classroom work that I saw varied from highly structured question-and-answer work via free-ranging discussion to independent projects. Even within the structured lessons there seemed to be a good deal of freedom, for instance in a closely directed computer class, where most of the students were following the teacher's instructions minute by minute, one was typing out poetry from a book, and another was doing something of his own on his machine, but stopping from time to time to help his neighbour who was having difficulty.

Lourdes Lugo, a powerful, lively teacher, told me of children arriving with a reading age of ten from the regular system and learning fast as soon as they understand that they can. When I first heard her teaching (from well outside her classroom) I had the impression that she was using her loud voice to dominate her students and to keep them in awe of her. Later, when I sat in on one of her history classes, I got a very different picture. There was a great deal of interest, questioning and discussion, and events from the past were clearly related to the present.

One topic that arose was the way attitudes to violence have changed over the centuries. Students were disgusted by the idea of torture and executions as a spectacle, and Lugo told them how a few years ago she had been driving a school bus when a man in the street just outside the school had seized another man by the hair, pulled his head back and cut it right off with a machete. Four girls in the bus had fainted, people were sick, and Lugo was shaking, trying to drive the bus away but stuck in a traffic jam. Although many of the students have been involved in gang violence, there is plainly no feeling within the school that violence is acceptable.

Sitting in the canteen as the students arrived one morning, I saw Lugo reading out snippets from her newspaper, and later walking round the room with it rolled up to hit at those who responded wrongly to her questions about homework. Everyone loved it. I saw her wrestling with one of the big, nineteen-year-old boys while he tried to shake her off without hurting her. Both of them were helpless with laughter. I heard "Capital Punishment", her item on the agenda for the Unity meeting, announced as, "Lugo wants to introduce capital punishment for coming to school late," and heard the laughter and then the respectful silence as she talked about the number of people on Death Row in Chicago and Illinois, many of whom had been wrongfully convicted. The mutual trust between staff and students is obvious and impressive.

This mutual trust, the cheerfulness and the laughter, sad to say, damage the school's reputation. Andreina told me how.

When they ask me, "What school do you go to?" they look at me differently. They're like, "Oh, you go to that school." They're like, "That's not a school, it's a playground." But it's not, you know, they've never been here, they don't know how things work here. I mean I'm always defending the school when somebody comes up to me and tells me, "Oh, you go to that Puerto Rican High, they're just terrorists. They teach you how to make bombs." It's not true. Whatever the political prisoners are accused of is not what they teach here. They are very caring. It's like a family.

The Unity Class

It's like a family. And as in a family, everyone has influence on the way things are run. Twice a week there is a session that the school calls a Unity Class, and I would call a school meeting. Everyone collects in the central hall to discuss an agenda proposed by individual students and staff. One of the weekly meetings is chaired by Marvin, and the other by a student.

At the meeting chaired by Marvin during the week I was there the agenda was, "Attendance. Physical exam. New Tutors. Bowlorama. Sophomore Group (Joel). Student point (Valeria). Some concerns: computers, class prep, general behaviour." In the event there was also a birthday greeting for one of the students, and Jesse read out a poem written by a student who did not want to read herself, but stood beside him while he read. The meeting ended with a rendering of La Borinqueña, the Puerto Rican national anthem, accompanied by Jesse on the maracas and Marvin on the cowbell.

The agenda for the other meeting, chaired by two students, included a welcome back to a student and her new baby, a welcome to a new student, details about a basketball tournament and a proposed poetry anthology, and the item that was listed as "Lugo suggests death penalty". Afterwards I asked Esmeralda whether she felt she had any say in how the school was run.

Actually we have a lot of say. In my first year in this school we had what's called a retreat, that's when the whole school goes out to camp at Camp White Eagle, and we had a Unity.

Here we were briefly interrupted by Carlos, her baby, who wanted the microphone again.

Yeah, we had a Unity at the camp, and they were asking us what we wanted to make different for this year that was coming. That would be my third year of high school. We told them we had a group of Mexicans here, and we heard all about Puerto Rico, and Puerto Rican history, and all of that, and we wanted Mexican history in a new class, because we didn't really have the slightest idea of our history. And we did, we did get a Mexican history teacher here, and it was an unforgettable class. We would have our Unities and we would tell the students, "Did you know that Hallowe'en in Mexico is actually the Day of the Dead?", and we had a shrine, and we brought pictures of our deceased, and we put up bread and water and the things that they liked to eat. And we had a lot of fun in that class. It was just great. And for extra credit we either had to cook some Mexican food, or we had to bring some bit of literature. And some other students, they got other classes that they wanted. Or they got to hear more about material that they were interested in. So we do have a lot of say in the school.

I asked about rules, such as the rule about smoking, and the rule that said you couldn't bring food upstairs.

I'm pretty sure a lot of students would like to change the rule about smoking but as we have the children downstairs there really can't be smoking around here. But smoking isn't very good for your health in the first place, so . . . But I don't smoke. And the food rule was sponsored by the students, because people used to eat on the sofas, and they used to leave things like stains or grease and stuff like that. People would go and sit on the sofas and it would be all over their pants. It was talked over in Unity and the rule was decided upon.

Most schools that are brave enough to share decision-making with their students retreat gradually towards conventionality, but Marvin told me that he would like to see the students being given more responsibility for decisions.

Benefits

How do the students feel they have benefited from the school?

I came not wanting to study, and in here the teachers are young and it motivates you more. You feel like, "Oh, they're young, and they're already teaching. I can do something that young."

Andreina

This is really not what you would call a school – it's more like a second home for most of us. It really opens our eyes to see the world and to see the government the way it really is. It helps us see how much we are being

Students at work

oppressed, and how much we've been taught in the regular schools that the government is for the people – for the rich white people. And we're taught to say if we think something is not good – if we see injustice, to do something about it.

Esmeralda

Instead of a gang giving a gun to a kid, why can't they give him a book? There are better ways to make money, there are better ways to help the community, instead of killing everybody in the community. You know, they're killing innocent people for things that they don't have nothing to do with. And I was part of this once. But now I try to better myself and I try to better all the shorties around me, all the youngsters around me, that were my age when I started out. I try to better them, I try to feed them some information, try to feed them some knowledge, instead of having them out there killing each other and me not caring. Because I do care, because I see myself when I see them.

Alguien

I feel my mind is more expanded compared to other people, how they think. A lot of people out there are very narrow-minded and in here they teach about so many different things. I do know more than other people when it comes to political things, and not just political things – things that are happening in the world.

Andreina

My main focus is I want to go to school, I want to major in English, and that'll be like my first couple of steps into getting where I want to be, because I can't say I've decided exactly where I want to be or who I want to be. I have such a wide variety to choose from, you know, why let it all go to waste? Definitely I'm going to do something with acting and I'm going to take that a step further and I'm going to take writing a step further and all the performances and all that, I'm definitely going to take it a step further. But I'm not going to forget my main goal, which is major in English.

Ada

I'm graduating this year, and I'm intending to go on to college. Have to see how that works with the baby. And after that I want to be a doctor, so I'll have to manage time for the baby and study and all of that.

Esmeralda

In one single rush of words Ada described the respect for young people that is so often forgotten in schools where the authority of adults takes precedence. And she not only described it, she also explained exactly why it is so important.

The difference between this school and other schools is that at least in this school I can say with my experiences, I've had a voice. I could come into school and say, "This is what I see wrong with the school, and this is what I feel should change, and this is what I think I should do," and I don't get laughed at. I won't get turned out.

My teachers are actually civil to me, and look at my good points and tell me, "OK, look, these are good points," and actually acknowledge my good points, look at my bad points and point them out to me, because a lot of times when you're young you don't realise. You figure, "OK, this is going to work like this," and you overlook things that are available. You don't really pay attention to them and you need somebody to point that out to you.

A lot of time adults, you know, they see teenagers, they see young kids trying to make a point and instead of trying to help us make a point, they make it look like we have no point at all, they make it look like we don't even know what we're talking about. And that's not good, because, see, we're the youth, we're tomorrow's future, we're the ones who are going to be – the torch is going to be handed on to us.

How are we supposed to run the world and have everything running right if we don't have the encouragement we need to go forward? We don't have what it is that we need, and adults use that against us, and they make it seem like, "OK, you can't never do that," and "You can't do this," and "You aren't ever going to be able to live up to me," or "You're never going to be able to handle responsibility." It's not because we're not able to handle responsibility, it's because the adults are not showing us responsibility, the adults are not showing us, "This is what you have to do." The examples that our teachers would set were, like, you're supposed to be racist, you're supposed to turn your back on your race.

That's public school and here in this school I got a chance to be myself without no strings attached. I could be myself, I don't have to hide nothing. And I'm truly myself, and even being myself, you know, just being OK, plain old Ada, who happens to be a teenager, who happens to go out and have fun, who happens to have a lot of friends and all that stuff, also writes poetry, also performs, also does this. I might have my points where I might not be so much of an adult because I'm still a kid, but there's other times in my life when I'm not a little kid any more. At least in this school they acknowledge that fact. I'm not a little kid for some things. I might be a kid for other things, because, yeah, I'm a teenager, you know, I'm not quite an adult yet, but at least they acknowledge that I have made efforts, have done something, and in a lot of places people just get overlooked, it's like it's there and nobody pays attention.

When the school moved to Division Street it was not going to change its underlying approach, but for Carlos the old building stood for the Dr. Pedro Albizu Campos Puerto Rican High School, and his lament for the building shows how much it meant to him.

I am going to be sad when they throw this building down. I am going to be sad. I mean it's like a part of me. It has helped me, it has given me opportunities. I don't want to leave this school. They're gonna throw it down when I finish high school. I'm going to be really sad, I tell you. I'm going to miss everybody in the school, everybody, every teacher, every student, every girl, everything.

It is easy to see why.

Moo Baan Dek, Thailand

Introduction

Rajani and Pibhop Dhongchai founded Moo Baan Dek in 1979. They wrote this on the occasion of the school's tenth anniversary:

> *In the beginning, we had 20 children ranging in age from four to ten, including our own two children, Ou and Eh. The first child to arrive went by the nickname of Ek. He came from the slum of Dindaeng. Ek was a maltreated child. His mother transferred her hatred of life to Ek throughout the first six years of his life. He was badly beaten repeatedly. Ek's mother confessed that she even used a knife to chase after him. "I don't know why, but when I get mad I lose control of myself. Sometimes I'd beat him with the broom until he became silent. He'd stop crying and stare at me. I'd beat him even harder for defying me."*
>
> *Ek's mother beat him until defiance and hatred showed clearly through his eyes and behaviour.*
>
> *We continued to take in children who displayed signs of defiance, aggression, and would swear when upset. Some of those children came from the slum under the Bangkok-Noi Bridge, some from the Klong-Toey slum, and from other slums in Bangkok. The forms of violence included not only beating with brooms but also cutting with small fruit knives, stamping with the feet, washing open wounds with salt water and forcing beaten children to sit in smoke. One of the most severe cases came from the Klong-Toey slum. The child was often hit on the head with a fruit-knife, which caused brain damage and nervous disorders. The worst case was a little girl who was raped since she was three and had contracted syphilis. She was afraid of men and darkness, was always fearful, and often screamed when left in the dark. Her defences were abusive language and destructive behaviour; she would bully anyone weaker. Some children from the country were beaten as well, and some were put into jars and dumped into rivers.*
>
> *The reason we often had this kind of children was because their parents did not want them. The parents blamed the children for their misbehaviour; they believed it was the children's doing, and not the result of their own actions. Even raped children were thought to have asked for it. Children were believed to be bad. But we provided them with a different kind of care, put them in a natural environment, fed them ample food, didn't subject them to such authoritarian adults, gave them love and kindness, and filled them with warmth. We granted them greater rights of participation to such an extent that the children often claimed, "This is my right." These children will take a turn*

for the better, if we are patient enough to give them the opportunity to change, and to try to understand them.

In 1999 the 150 children at Moo Baan Dek were classified by reasons of intake:

Abuse	*29*
Abandonment	*25*
Broken home	*54*
Homelessness (runaway)	*16*
Orphanage	*26*

Many of these children came from the worst imaginable backgrounds, and what is more, as I learnt from staff and children there, those backgrounds were often harshly authoritarian. If it were true that children who have been brought up by authoritarian parents will never be able to behave responsibly unless they are under imposed discipline, then Moo Baan Dek would have been bound to fail.

The school is modelled on Summerhill, A. S. Neill's school in Suffolk, England, which is based on the interwoven principles of freedom and self-government. At Moo Baan Dek these principles are given a Buddhist interpretation.

Rajani described the twin origins of the school's philosophy in a talk she gave in 1981, when the school had only been running for two years.

According to Buddhist belief, each human being possesses within him/herself both low and high instincts, that is – primitive instincts and perfect, human virtue.

Low instincts or primitive instincts originate from ignorance, having vice as its driving force.

High instincts originate from knowledge and wisdom, having kindness as its driving force.

The problem is then:

"What can we do to arrange the environment or external factors that would cultivate wisdom and kindness into the human heart while reducing ignorance and vice, so that life is led to its ultimate aim; being in harmony with nature, and having **wisdom** *as life's guide and* **kindness** *as its inspiration."*

In the later article I have already quoted, Pibhop and Rajani defined Neill's contributions like this:

The fundamental concepts were freedom, self-government, and a concern for the total person including the physical and emotional factors as well as the

Bathing in the river Kwae

mind. Specifically, this meant a freedom to choose to learn, an organisational structure which reduced authoritarianism by reducing the authority of the adults and by increasing the authority of the children. It also meant building relationships between adults and children based on freedom, equality and mutual respect, and by using love as the binding agent.

A third powerful influence was the Dhongchais' belief in the healing power of natural surroundings.

We believe that every school should be near a river. In the absence of rivers, there should be a pool to provide the children with an opportunity to play in the water. From our experience, access to fresh water and to growing plants has therapeutic effects on emotionally disturbed children. These elements in nature provide support for the inner self, which is the "heart matter", an aspect of education and child care which our country often lacks. Essential activities which relax depressed or aggressive emotions include playing with soil, water, plants, and animals, acting in plays, dancing, singing and enjoying art. However, these activities must be conducted freely, and not as a course with fixed goals and time limits. Activities which require competition and evaluation and are systematised are tiresome for the children.

First impressions

I had heard of Moo Baan Dek many years before we visited it. I finally met Rajani and Pibhop at the International Democratic Education Conference in Tokyo in 2000, and was delighted when they agreed to my request to visit them.

My wife, Lynette, and I were guests there for a week in January 2001. We were met at the airport by Pipob Udomittipong, his wife and young son, and the driver of the school minibus. Pipob, who we soon came to know as Ped, to distinguish him from Pibhop Dhongchai, the founder, acted as our interpreter and guide throughout our visit. He took us first to the offices of the Foundation For Children, the organisation founded by the Dhongchais of which Moo Baan Dek is a part, to fetch Rajani and take her back to the school with us. She had been taking part in a morning of meetings, and was fast asleep on the sofa. Through the open doors of the next building we could see small children, also sleeping. They were being looked after in the Foundation's malnutrition unit, where children are cared for when their families can no longer afford food.

The drive to the school, some 150 kilometres away, was broken by a visit to the bridge over the river Kwae. Even though we were still at a tourist site with strong associations for Britons, I was beginning to feel that we were escaping from the vapid anonymity of international air travel and were starting to emerge into a different culture. There was a restaurant floating on bundles of bamboo, moored to the bank of the river. There were a great many scooters, often driven by young men with girls sitting sidesaddle on the back. We ate Thai ices and jackfruit.

When we reached Moo Baan Dek we seemed to have come another step away from the cosmopolitan world of Bangkok. We turned off the tarmac of the main road and bumped down a sandy track between bamboos, palms and banana trees. The school owns sixty acres of rough woodland which it had bought cheaply because the land had been overused for sugar production, and was thought to be infertile. The track led down past a football field and a basketball court, barely perceptible in the dusk, through the trees to an open space with buildings scattered round it. Ped's family got out of the minibus there, and Rajani drove on with us to one of the houses for guests, where she provided us with a large bowl of fruit and biscuits and made sure that we had mosquito nets properly erected.

The main rooms, as in all the other houses, were on the first floor. We reached them up a wooden staircase on the outside of the building. The ground floor had a storeroom or two, but most of it was a kind of veranda, a shady place to keep out of the sun. This is a traditional Thai style and has the additional advantage that if your house is flooded your main living quarters are above the water. Modern conveniences were electric light, a fan and a water-cooler. There was only cold running water, but in January the weather is hot enough for a cold shower to be welcome. Our mattresses were the only furniture. All the light bulbs were energy-saving, in keeping with the emphasis on environmental responsibility. The floors in two of our rooms were of polished wood, but the floor outside the shower room was made of flat stones bedded in sand. The window in the shower room was just an opening in the roof above the washbasin. It looked out over one end of the vegetable gardens; anybody working there could look in, if they chose to. We had lizards on the ceiling and on one occasion a long-legged pink frog in the lavatory bowl. It hopped out and disappeared before we could think how to get it out of the house.

It was already dark when we arrived, so after supper in the guest dining-room near the kitchens and a brief visit to the other guest-house, where we met Pibhop Dhongchai's mother, who was sitting contentedly in a room full of lively children, we went to our own house to try to recover from jet lag.

The next morning was Saturday. We breakfasted alone in the guests' dining-room at 7.30 and then sat outside on benches at tables sheltered from the sun by bamboo roofs to watch what was going on. There were several buildings scattered round the area – the kitchens and dining-room, the library and offices, the nursery school building and playground and a square courtyard, open in our direction, surrounded by three boarding-houses. The library and central office was a hexagonal two-storey building with a balcony running round the upper floor; the roof hung well over the walls to give shade. There were trees between the buildings making the whole complex seem only a part of the grey-green woodland, where the sunlight speckled the ground through the foliage. There were many more boarding-houses and classrooms hidden away down paths among the trees.

It was plainly a children's world around us. Children as young as four were making their independent and purposeful ways hither and thither. There were no adults to be seen, but there were many friendly dogs and puppies, and unworried hens and chickens pecking up what had been spilt from breakfast bowls. At a table near where I was sitting, a girl of about six was organising a group of boys to play a game which involves everyone piling up their fists and then chanting a rhyme. At a certain point in the rhyme the bottom fist goes flat, and the whole column drops a little. When all the hands are flat, the rhyme changes, and the hands are removed one at a time, each time slapping the hand underneath. This was not a completely easy game, and soon one of the boys lost interest and came over to me and said, "Good morning." I said good morning back, and there was a little burst of good mornings and how are yous. One boy came and showed me a balloon, which he correctly named as "balloon".

Most of the teenage children were going off to the rice fields to harvest the rice, and a crowd collected, waiting for the lorry. It was a peaceful and relaxed crowd, even though the lorry had broken down and was late. It arrived eventually, an open-backed lorry with a canopy over it and seats at the sides with bars to lean against. About forty children got into it, and those sitting on the back looked pretty perilous as the lorry bounced over the track towards the road. It reminded me of the days when we were less safety-conscious in Britain, children used to ride on tractors and no-one wore a helmet on a bicycle. It looked fun.

Two groups of smaller boys came in sight. One group was sweeping the sand off the paving outside the central office building opposite to where I was sitting. When they had finished that, they went on to sweep the sandy area itself – perhaps clearing it of leaves, or hens' messes. They had a woman supervising them, but the other group, who were collecting rubbish with a slightly older boy carrying a plastic bin into which they put their finds, were not supervised. They seemed to be having fun, as if it was more of a treasure-hunt than a chore.

Rajani and Ped came out and told us that we should also go to the rice fields, as that was where most of the school would be. The event turned out to be rich in information about the school, and must be described in detail. We were driven there in the smart school minibus, stopping on the way to drop off a group of staff at the local primary school, which was being used as a polling station for the general election. The primary school, too, was interesting, but more of that later.

The four rice-fields belonging to Moo Baan Dek were part of a big area of rice about forty kilometres away. Neither Lynette nor I had any idea how rice was harvested, or even what it looked like as it grew. It turned out to look much like oats, but growing in little clumps rather than rows. Twenty or thirty of the children and the adults who had come with them were working forward independently across the field, all wearing big sunhats. Others were preparing the lunch, resting, or fishing. (I didn't see the fishing, but the fish turned up at lunch-time. They came from the irrigation ditches between the fields, where there were so many of them that they could be scooped out by hand.) We watched the harvest for a while.

The reapers all had sickles. The technique was to separate out a clump of stalks, to hold it with one hand and cut it a foot or so from the ground. Behind the reapers other people collected the small bundles of rice into sheaves and tied them together with stalks. Rajani was already working with the others by the time we reached the field, indistinguishable from the crowd.

After a while we were both offered sickles, and we worked for a while, rather inefficiently. Ped, who had never cut rice before, was learning too. It was getting towards midday, and the number of reapers was gradually diminishing. Then there was a call from behind us that lunch was ready, and we returned to a bank near where a group of adults and children had been preparing the food in a little grove on the top of some raised ground.

We sat with Rajani and Ped on the scratchy dry grass and were joined by various children from time to time, but most of the teenagers sat together in the shade a little way away. We ate rice from small cylindrical baskets, and crisps from ordinary plastic packets, and meat and green vegetables in a sauce. There was also another dish of vegetables in a sauce that was said to be too hot for us, and tiny raw fish in another sauce that was said to be too hot for us, and occasional little bits of slightly larger fish, roasted in an open fire, and fruit like huge peanuts in long shells, which had tasty red flesh round hard, nutty kernels. You helped yourself to rice from the communal baskets with your fingers, rolled it into a ball and dipped up as much as you wanted of the sauces and other dishes. Children frequently came to give us glasses of water or particular delicacies. They would sit down close to Rajani and talk to her affectionately without either awe or ostentation.

There were sickles lying all over the place, and when one of the workers who had been helping with the fire wanted his machete, he asked an eight-year-old girl to fetch it for him. (The term "worker" needs some explanation. As well as teachers and houseparents at Moo Baan Dek there are a dozen families who live in the grounds and work as cooks, builders, maintenance men and drivers, and also work in the gardens and on the rice fields. Their status is similar to that of the other staff; they attend the school meetings, they are the experts on traditional methods of agriculture and they take the youngest children to live with them in their own families.) The girl sent to fetch the machete took it out of its sheath and brought it to him, but he told her she should have brought it in the sheath, so she went back, put machete in the sheath and returned with it. He used it to sharpen a stick to roast fish on, and the girl then cooked several of the bigger fish over the fire. This ancient procedure was brought into the present-day by the fact that she was wearing a Lion King tee shirt.

As the meal drew to a close, some of the smaller children clambered onto the lorry and used the bars as a climbing frame. The older ones rested in the shade. It was extraordinarily peaceful and pleasant, and when I commented to Ped about how calm everybody seemed, he said it was a cultural difference – Thai people from the countryside were relaxed and behaved like this naturally.

Rajani explained to us that the rice was harvested in the traditional way because the heavy tractors that some of the farmers used were damaging the soil. We heard more about ecologically sound agriculture later in our visit, but this was our first encounter with it.

I asked her what she felt about the children who had been helping with the reaping but had stopped well before lunch-time. It was absolutely right, she said. Their bodies told them that they needed rest, and it was proper for them to obey their natural needs. This trust and generosity was illustrated again later.

The theory seemed to be justified by the fact that work started after lunch in much the same informal way as it had stopped beforehand. Children began to go back to the fields again, some to continue reaping, and the bigger boys to collect the sheaves and stack them in the lorry. They collected the sheaves on long poles, which they carried over their shoulders. It took three people to manage a pole, one to carry it and the others to load three sheaves on each end. Girls were standing in the lorry, stacking the sheaves as they arrived. There was no visible organiser. It may possibly have been adults who started to move back to work, but no-one gave any instruction; it just happened that before long everyone was busy again.

We left to come back to the school and sleep again, but the lorry did not get back till about seven in the evening.

The absence of pressure was illustrated again in a different way when I later interviewed Michaela Jørgensen, a Danish volunteer who had been teaching English at Moo Baan Dek for about a year. Unfortunately there were few of the other staff who spoke more than a little English, but Mikka was extremely helpful. It was useful that she, as a European, was surprised by the same cultural differences as we were, and as someone who had spent some years in Thailand, and spoke the language, she was able to explain them. I asked her how people helped her to fit in when she first arrived, and this is her reply.

They helped me to feel comfortable here. They helped me to settle into my house, and to talk to people, but nobody actually told me when I was going to teach or where. And I found it strange, I was like, "Well, I come here and you have to give me a schedule or something." I didn't know a lot about the school and the philosophy of the school, so I just waited and thought, "OK, I'll just hang around until I find out what they want," because they are the ones who are going to be taught, right? But they were waiting for me, and that is what they do with all the children. They were waiting for me to feel good, and find what I wanted to do and what would make me happy, because if I wasn't happy then I wouldn't be able to give anything to anyone. Like the children have to fit in with their classes or their teacher, and sometimes they don't want to go to the assembly, and they run around playing instead. I did that for two or three weeks and I had a lot of fun, and I thought, "Well, if they don't tell me to teach I'm not going to press it, because I'm having a good time, right?" So I had a lot of fun, but then I thought, "Oh, OK, I'll put up a notice," because I kept asking for a schedule and they didn't give it to me. Anyway, I put up a notice, "If anyone wants to study English, come to my house," and then some time after, the children started coming and I started teaching them.

That was quite a funny experience, because I was just like the children, and they said everybody was like this, but you have some people who have a few days and then they are ready to do what they want, and I just didn't know exactly what I really wanted, and I liked to do other things too, so I went to the gardens and to the rice-fields and all that. I felt that for me I had to be comfortable with the people that I was going to teach and know them a little bit before, maybe, that is my nature, so when I started teaching them it was the right time.

Pibhop and Rajani described how the process sometimes took rather longer for some of the children who arrived at Moo Baan Dek.

Teachers are required to teach as set in the timetable, from 9.00 a.m. to 12.00 noon, whether or not students attend. In practice, we always ask or suggest that students attend classes after three years of play and therapeutic activities.

Three years! It shows not only how deeply damaged some of the children are, but also how vast the patience of the staff is. My impression was that most children started very much more promptly, but the freedom from expectation is still astonishing.

Buddhism and the Summerhill system

Moo Baan Dek was set up to be a Buddhist version of Summerhill. This seems astonishing at first. Summerhill is wrongly associated with self-indulgence and disorder, and Buddhism is associated with asceticism and calm. We soon came to see that there is in practice no marked difference when it comes to living with children.

The belief underlying the Summerhill approach is that the child is basically good, and it is the mistaken efforts of parents and society that distort this natural goodness. If you allow children to grow in freedom from the beginning, this distortion can be avoided, and up until the age of ten or so children who are already damaged by their upbringing can recover in a free environment. A. S. Neill used to give amateur psychotherapy when the school first started, but he soon abandoned it because he found that it was the environment itself that was therapeutic.

Some Buddhists would agree that human nature is good, and is only changed by defilement in life, but others say that it is both good and evil. At Moo Baan Dek they remain open-minded, but in practice what happens is very much the same as at Summerhill. The children govern their own freedom, discover purpose and show wisdom.

I asked Rajani in what ways Moo Baan Dek manifested its Buddhist philosophy and she told me that it is firstly in the general ethos of the place. It is friendly. It is welcoming for the children. This is one of the main teachings of Buddhism, she said. You must become *Kalayanamitra* which means "good friends".

An example is the relationship between teachers and children. This relationship must be equal. In Buddhist tradition, in the *Sangha*, the community of monks, everyone, once he becomes a monk, is equal regardless of race, regardless of caste. Buddhism, she reminded me, originated in India, which was dominated by the caste system. Just as the Buddha once said that all monks are equal in his monasteries, so all teachers and children are equal in Moo Baan Dek. They all have the same opportunity to realise their potential.

Another Buddhist teaching concerns the role of the teacher. Learning can take place only when the child becomes self-motivated. Teachers cannot force anyone to learn; they can perhaps interest them in learning but force serves no purpose. There must be self-motivation, which Buddhists call *Chanda*. And on the teacher's side what is needed is *Viriya*, the right effort to help the student to implant his own motivation.

Rajani enlarged on the practical aspects of the effort to create self-motivation in the children.

Voting at a school meeting

We know our limits, we are not able to cope with every background, we are not able to convince the student who comes from too difficult a background, we are not able to change that background, so the work here begins with the teacher. We help the students to have faith in the adults and to trust the adults, and once they trust the adults, the adults can help them to do something. Once they begin to undertake any activities we try to shift the faith to the work itself, so the student will have faith in the work itself, not in any personality, and at that point the teacher should step back so that children can take advice about how to do the work but not obey his personality.

We are also able to allow the students to grow naturally in natural surroundings. We make good use of the river. And we provide them with activities which are non-exploitative, and also non-violent. And another aspect of the environment that we try to control is media. We keep trying to provide a good creative media.

And so overall this environment depends on community life and on top of this we go on the principle of **Brahmavihara Dhamma**. *This is a Buddhist teaching. Number one is* **Metta**, *loving-kindness, which applies in normal situations. Then when the children are in need we have to extend to them compassion –* **Karuna** *– to help them out of their suffering. The third quality is* **Mudita**, *sympathetic joy, to appreciate the children's achievements. And lastly,* **Upekkha**, *equanimity, which I would like to compare to non-interference in Neill's Summerhill School. In other words, we don't interrupt the children unless they express a need for our help, or unless they show some signs of needing some help. And once they show some signs of asking for help, compassion, or* **Karuna**, *should be applied.*

The Buddhist respect for the environment is shown in the agricultural methods used at the school. They follow the methods of the Japanese ecologist and natural farmer Masanobu Fukuoka, which means that they avoid using artificial pesticides and fertilisers, and take care to grow crops which complement each other. It is for the same sort of reason that they use no machinery in their rice fields.

Contrasts

The first surprise that children get when they arrive at Moo Baan Dek is to find that they are assured of three good meals every day. Sometimes new children cannot believe that there is going to be enough food for everybody, and fight to get in the front of the queue. They are also given shelter, two sets of clothes and medical treatment when they need it. All these are things that new students at Summerhill would take for granted. They would indeed find two sets of clothes quite inadequate, and would be unhappy at having to sleep on the floor rather than in beds.

The difference between the expectations of the children at Moo Baan Dek and the children at Summerhill seems so great that it is astonishing that a single approach can serve them both.

Thai society is extremely hierarchical. There are eleven different words for "you", all indicating differences of status. There is a word, "krengjai", which means consideration for the feelings of others; however, when it is applied to attitudes towards superiors, it also includes the ideas of obedience, humility and respect. The normal way of greeting someone is with the *wai*, holding your hands in front of you with the palms together, and bowing; the depth of the bow, and the height at which you hold your hands, are both socially significant, and servants may actually sink to their knees. Within the family the younger children are expected to obey their elders, and the older children are expected to accept responsibility for the behaviour of the younger ones.

Thais are said to detest violence, but this does not extend to school discipline; the government's introduction of a ban on corporal punishment is contested with some heat. A teacher, quoted in the Bangkok Post, said, "Some parents spoil their children and pressure schools and teachers not to punish them. Still, I believe more than half of the parents want us to continue caning their children in a constructive way. ... If our children misbehave, we'd like to see them punished, including caning, so that they learn to differentiate right from wrong. This has been the way we have reared children in our society for centuries and I strongly feel that it should be maintained."

Summerhill has always known that children understand the difference between right and wrong, whether or not they have been "caned in a constructive way". When it was founded in the 1920s caning, constructive or not, was taken for granted in most schools, just as it is now in Thailand. Even now it is favoured by many parents in Britain, so perhaps this contrast is not as marked as we would hope.

A stronger contrast is in the attitude to the monarchy. There are portraits of the King wherever you go in Thailand. When we were travelling by plane, Lynette began licking stamps to put them on her postcards; her Thai neighbour told that this was disrespectful, as the King's face was on the stamps. Instead of using her tongue she should have licked her finger and used that.

We spent a short time at the local primary school which was being used as a polling station, waiting for the people with us to cast their votes. The central building was built of concrete, and had a balcony on the first floor where the words, "Morality, discipline, knowledge", were displayed in English and Thai. The classrooms were spread around the site. They had roofs and only one wall, where the blackboard was. There were tables and benches, five benches to accommodate probably thirty to forty children, which looked like a squash. The grounds were big and full of plants, except for the large playing-field, and there were several decorative pools of water. There was also a shrine to the Queen Mother, whose birthday it would have been, had she lived. A government edict had gone out that every school in Thailand must build such a temple – in this case four pillars with a dome on the top, perhaps eight feet high and five feet square, with a display board with photographs and information. Every school is of course full of pictures of the King, and has the national flag flying outside. The flag is blue, white and red – blue for the monarchy, white for religion and red for blood, which means patriotism. (At Moo Baan Dek I did not notice any pictures of the King, or any shrine to his mother, but the national flag was hoisted every day.)

Within this society it is difficult for Moo Baan Dek to find and retain sympathetic staff. Many teachers leave because they cannot accept equal status with the children, or tolerate the occasional swearing or aggressive behaviour. Pibhop and Rajani started by employing teachers from ordinary training colleges but found many of them did not share their progressive views. Now they are more inclined to take graduates from other disciplines, such as law and social science, but such people sometimes have difficulty in relating to small children. Others are frustrated by their inability to get quick results, or by the rules against smoking, drinking or having private TV sets, which apply to the staff as well as the children.

Similarities

When I asked Mikka, the young Dane, what attracted her so much about the place, she said, "The nature, the children, everybody being equal." I asked exactly how equal everybody was, and she said, "We have rules that everybody has to follow, and everybody has to come over to the school meeting. Sometimes the teachers or the housemothers might feel they are superior, they have more power, but that is only to remind the children of the rules that everybody has to keep. Rajani is superior because she made the place. Everybody is thankful to her and respects her a lot and listens very much to her, but she is living under the same rules that the rest of us are living under here, so actually it is only because she is respected that she is actually superior." This was certainly confirmed by the way the children approached her at lunch-time in the rice fields.

Several children told me during interviews that they regarded Rajani as their mother, even though they lived in houses with other housemothers to care for them. And yet when we were there the relationship between children and the other adults also seemed thoroughly friendly and affectionate.

In their tenth anniversary account of the school Pibhop and Rajani included the description that follows.

We believe that both the children and the adults are members of the Moo Baan Dek community, each having his or her own defined responsibility and each having similar rights and privileges. The only difference is the work responsibility of each person.

The rights and privileges begin from variation in responsibility. We all have the right to live a happy life, but such happiness should not be taken advantage of, or violate the rights and freedoms of others. As such, everyone must have his or her own work responsibility in order to lead a happy life without infringing upon others, or upon nature. The work responsibility must be freely chosen, and this choice must be preceded by a sense of freedom of the inner self. Therefore, children who have been controlled by authoritarianism, some of whom were physically hurt and emotionally scarred, have deep emotional problems. Such a child likes to hurt others, to take advantage of others, and is selfish and mean. These children's problems are so overpowering they do not know themselves or their capabilities. If the child continues to live in an authoritarian environment, the oppression and the emotional scars will never heal; they will remain deeply rooted mental complexes. The only way to treat this is to let the child open up the emotional wound, in an atmosphere of freedom, love and warmth, such that he or she is not afraid to show emotional scars. Then, we begin the healing process with therapeutic activities, controlling the adults' behaviour as well as the environment.

The emphasis on work responsibility would be foreign to Summerhill, but as you read on you see that this work responsibility is to be freely chosen as a result of a sense of inner freedom. Just as we saw no compulsion in the rice-fields, or in the groups of children sweeping the paths or scavenging for rubbish, so we did not feel there was any authority forcing the children to work in the vegetable gardens, or to help with the cooking. The tasks seemed to be accepted without question. Elsewhere in the same account Rajani and Pibhop wrote, "Work is also an activity, but it should not be treated as a duty, for a child cannot concentrate for long. A duty would be a burden, and that is no fun for children."

The daily routine

The day starts with work in the gardens at 6.30. The gardens are extensive, and tended with astonishing care and enthusiasm. On our first morning we saw children aged five or six squatting down to pick out tiny weeds in neat rows of vegetables, others planting and another group collecting armfuls of spring onions. The children work contentedly, the younger ones with older children overseeing them to make sure everything is being done properly. As well as the main school gardens there is a plot for each boarding-house to grow what it needs. Several of the children I interviewed said they particularly enjoyed the farming, and a girl called Mai explained why she did. She liked the exercise, she said, she liked learning how plants grow so that she can answer the teachers, and she liked to do something useful which provided food.

At half past seven there is breakfast and then supposedly at half past eight there is assembly, but at that time people were still eating their breakfasts or tidying up or collecting their schoolbooks, and the bell was not rung until about a quarter to nine. This is another indication of the lack of tension in the general atmosphere.

While we were waiting for the bell to ring a group of small children collected round Lynette, and one small boy began to teach her tricks with her fingers, rather like "Here's the church and here's the steeple." All went well until he began to show her a trick which involved poking a finger into a hole, and one of the girls interrupted, and insisted that he stopped. Little incidents like this contain a great deal of information: the children were happy to approach a stranger who did not speak their language and not only were they eager to make friends, but they had devised ways of doing so; nevertheless one of their number tried to make fun of Lynette by encouraging her to make some gesture that was presumably obscene; another child was determined to protect her from this mockery, and succeeded in doing so. All this time there were no members of staff in sight; the children were acting independently and took their freedom absolutely for granted.

Soon after the bell was rung, the children collected in the theatre, an open-sided building with a swept concrete floor, and suddenly the school became comparatively formal. Everyone took off their shoes before entering the space, but this was not unexpected, as you took off your shoes before entering any building. What was surprising was that they then formed up into lines, and sang the national anthem, while the national flag was slowly hoisted in front of them. This was followed by a prayer. Most of the younger children seemed indifferent to all this ceremony, and looked around for more interesting things to watch, but nevertheless they remained standing in their orderly lines. It was the teenagers who were most engaged in the rituals.

After the prayer the children were told to move into a circle, and played a few games which involved jumping in and out of shoes. Then they sat down and were supposed to meditate for a few minutes while the teacher running the assembly walked round the circle, speaking in a soothing voice. Some of the older children closed their eyes and seemed to be taking the meditation seriously, while others, particularly the younger ones, passed messages by making faces, and one, a known troublemaker, made a farting noise at which others laughed. The teacher, still speaking in her quiet, reassuring voice, told him he could leave if he did not want to take part, but he stayed.

Working in the vegetable gardens

After meditation they did a few simple yoga exercises. Quite a number did not join in with everything, although they all seemed to enjoy the exercise which involved everyone sitting facing in one direction around the circle and massaging the back of the person in front, and then relaxing forwards and backwards on top of their neighbours.

The whole occasion was surprising for two opposite reasons: firstly, because it was such an adult-directed, formal occasion; and, secondly, because so much chatting and inattention were allowed, apparently without comment.

The children then split up to go to their various classes. On our first day I only saw formal teaching with children working quietly from textbooks, but on other days there were classes out in the woods and around the different buildings. All the children are supposed to go to classes from nine until twelve, but if they don't want to they can do something else. "If a child does not come to a particular class for a long time," Mikka told me, "the teacher may say, 'Hey, don't you think it's time?' or tease them, maybe, or make something fun so the child will think, 'Wow, I missed that,' but will not say, 'You have to come.' They kind of wait for the child to come themself."

While I was visiting the upper primary classes, Lynette went to the nursery class, where they were using Montessori methods that they had first studied and introduced only a year or so previously. There were twenty-four children with three teachers. The children lined up outside the door before going in and sitting on the tiled floor with books, looking at their books and chatting. Then they gathered round one of the teachers to do rhymes and songs. These were followed by a short video about letters, and then the children moved into a second room where they had drawing books or sticker books. Children help themselves to these and pencils. There was a lot of chatter, and a certain amount of noise from outside.

Then activities became more varied. An easel was put up; there was a table with sticklebricks on it; beautiful mats were put on the floor for building blocks. There was much gluing and building and fixing, sometimes alone and sometimes collaboratively. A little girl picked up a magnifying glass and looked at her hand. There were jigsaws available, and sheets of coloured paper and scissors. Water play was set up on another table. The children appeared to flow from one activity to another without adult interference or direction, as if they had become used to a loose routine. The adults, however, seem to be clear about what is and is not acceptable or to be encouraged at any given moment. After a period of self-directed activity everyone was taken back to the video room for some films.

Although there was Montessori material being used there was more chat and interaction than is sometimes encouraged in a Montessori classroom, and there was great use of videos.

Working in the classroom

There were two or three noticeably older children among the group. Ped had told us that children move through the school at their own pace, and some of the children have severe learning difficulties. He had pointed out one seven-year-old who I had taken to be four or five, who he said could not yet talk. At the time, he was going off somewhere with a troop of other children, apparently accepted and content. Ped told us that there is no disgrace attached to going through the school at a different age to most other people.

Lynette wondered how the children who had become used to the self-directed Montessori system would adapt to the formal education in the classrooms to come, but apparently it is not the children who are going to have to adapt, but the formal education system. Already in the first class there is much more practical activity than there had been before the Montessori approach was introduced in the kindergarten.

Lunch was distributed at the central kitchen, unlike breakfast and supper, which were prepared and eaten in the separate boarding-houses.

After lunch the workshops were open, but when we were there they were not being much used. The choices normally available were computing, batik, weaving, dressmaking, English, electronics and pottery. The pottery teacher was away, though, in New Zealand learning English. There were perhaps a dozen children taking part. Ped said the other children were probably in their houses, reading, talking or sleeping. Some of the younger ones were in the library, watching cartoons on the television there.

Even in January the sun was hot, and even among the grey-trunked trees there was only a sprinkling of shade. After the rice had been left to dry for a day or two there was a group working on the basketball court, in spite of the heat, threshing the rice by using a rope between two sticks to grasp the sheaves, lift them above their heads and batter them down on the ground, again and again until all the grains were released.

At four o'clock every day there is a swimming session down at the dock on the river Kwae. The campus itself is fairly flat, but it is edged by the river, perhaps forty feet below. You reach the swimming area by passing through one of the workers' farmyards, occupied by chickens and dogs, and then descending a steep flight of stairs. Across the river are the forested hills immediately before the frontier to Burma.

Some of the housemothers come down to supervise, and there is always at least one older student or member of staff actually in the water to make sure no-one strays into danger. The depth and speed of the river vary according to the amount of water released from the big dam upstream from the school. The dock is a wooden platform that reaches out from the shore, four feet or more above the water, according to the amount of water in the river. You can jump or dive off the end, or you can climb down the steps beside it, or you can walk into the water from the shore. On the dock some of the children will be

In the weaving room

washing their clothes in big tubs. Some of them soap their hair while they stand on the dock and then rinse the soap out in the river. Some of the girls swim in what appears to be all their clothes, and there are dozens of naked small boys diving, splashing, pushing and laughing.

Even in January this is an important occasion every day. Bathing, I was told, releases tensions, allows energy to explode peacefully, distracts from anxiety and helps towards calm and contentment.

Supper is prepared and eaten in the different boarding-houses, and the evening is free. Ped took me round to show me what the houses were like, and where the children slept.

The houses are scattered about in the woods, and each one is built to a different design. In all of them the main rooms are upstairs, off a large, open, central space, which eliminates the need for corridors. Bedrooms, shower rooms, lavatories and kitchen all open off this central room, where there is a large table for eating and games and conversation. In most of the houses there is also a big balcony; I had long, quiet chats with Ped and Mikka on such balconies in the evening, with the lights from the house shining out on the surrounding trees.

The very youngest children, up to the age of four, live with the families of the workers, and the kindergarten children have a separate boarding-house. Until the age of twelve the houses include both boys and girls, but the teenagers are separated. The dormitories are more or less square, with just space for perhaps as many as eight thin mattresses on the tiled floor, and a corresponding number of drawers or lockers. I saw only two sample dormitories; one had nothing but graffiti on the walls, and the other was decorated with posters and pictures from magazines. One belonged to boys, and the other to girls. The smaller children, Ped told me, often prefer to sleep in one big pile, rather than on their separate bedding.

I saw one kitchen; this was where food was prepared for the dozen or so people who lived in the house. There were three calor gas rings, a sink, a large rack for plates and vegetables and one cupboard. There is a tap in the sink, but drinking water is kept separately. There were vegetables on the vegetable rack and a bunch of green bananas in one corner – not just a handful of them but a whole tall cluster. Most vegetables come from the organic gardens. Each house is given a little money to buy food, and some coupons for certain goods from the central kitchens. The children plan their own menus with the houseparents. Rice is provided free. The money and the coupons help the children to learn about housekeeping.

Lynette and I spent some time in the evening with Ped in the central room of the house where Mikka was living. The adults sat chatting at the main table, surrounded by children, mostly under nine, I would guess, playing draughts, drawing and colouring, working on join-the-dots pictures or playing with wooden bricks. When they finished what they were doing they all carefully put the equipment away again. Ped told us that one of them was his "enemy", often unmanageable and given to breaking windows; that evening he was sitting close beside him, and was quiet and busy. Two of the draughts-players, we were told, were also fond of breaking glass.

One draughts-player put the board away on a low shelf near me which was plainly not the right one, as the other games were on a much higher shelf. I asked Ped why this was, and he said it was because if the boy had put the game back on the right shelf, it would have involved climbing up on a chair so that his head was higher than my head, and that would have been insulting. When he had taken the game down Lynette had been sitting where I was now, and he had been brave enough to ask her for permission before climbing up; I was more inhibiting. This was an instance of Thai good manners going much further than what we were used to. An instance of the reverse occurred when I was allowed to hold a baby who was being looked after by one of the older students. She made some comment to a nearby friend, and they both laughed, so I asked Ped what had been said. Ped told me quite happily that she had said that my stomach made it look as though I was soon going to have a baby of my own, and we all laughed together. Although you must not allow your head to rise above the head of a superior, jokes about physical appearance are quite acceptable.

You could also watch videos in the meeting room, play with your friends, or read newspapers and watch television in the library. On our way back to our house we met three adolescent girls on one bicycle, shrieking with laughter as they whirled through the darkness.

Bedtime for the younger children is at nine o'clock, but many of them go to sleep before that. There is no kudos attached to staying up late. The older ones have no set bedtime, but they have to show up for garden work in the morning at 6.30, and for breakfast, if they want it, at 7.30.

The School Council

The School Council is a system which helps children and adults to learn the application of freedom, which will lead eventually to self-government. The failure of freedom in many cases was caused by ineffective application of it, and also by the unwillingness of people to cooperate. Freedom is an agreement among the people of that community as to the boundary of freedom set. Too great an emphasis on the public freedom may affect individual freedom, and vice versa. Thus, freedom must be within bounds, but such bounds must be collectively determined by members of the community.

Moo Baan Dek is made up of community members, both children and adults. We hold weekly meetings to determine the boundaries of community freedom. We also use the meetings to study conflicts among the members, as well as to define the lifestyle and some cultural aspects of the community. The assembly sets regulations to be observed in the community, and rescinds or modifies outdated regulations. ... It is true that sometimes mistakes do happen and the rules set may violate the individual rights of some people, but the children and adults can always correct the mistake in the following week. It seems incredible that the children would know and understand this, especially the really young children. But this happens, as long as we believe in the children. The adult's confidence in the child will lead the child to have confidence in the adult, and that mutual confidence will be reflected in the community.

Real Life at Moo Baan Dek, p. 69

So wrote Rajani and Pibhop. Unfortunately our travel arrangements meant that we missed Friday afternoon, when that all-important school meeting is held. However, we were still able to learn something about it.

The status of the meeting is illustrated by the fact that a special hall has been built to house it. The hall is roughly hexagonal, and lies on a slope, so that benches rise up naturally on three sides, facing towards the chairperson's position at the bottom. It looks rather like an old-fashioned science lecture-hall, where experiments could be observed by a large audience, though the raking is not quite so steep, and there are no desks to write on. There is room for all the children, teachers, houseparents and workers, and they are expected to attend. The chair is taken by a pupil, appointed at the end of the previous meeting. The agenda consists of announcements, reports from the Justice Committee (about which I shall say more later), discussion of problems the Justice Committee was not able to solve, and proposals for new rules or other changes. At the beginning of the meeting each house checks that all its members are present, or explains why they are not. During the meetings the youngest children are listened to with as much respect as the older members, and the adults have no special status.

Towards the end of our visit I interviewed some children, with Ped as translator, and I asked most of them what they thought of the meeting. Mai, a girl of about twelve, who had been at Moo Baan Dek for six years and had often taken the chair, felt that sometimes people took the meeting really seriously – this was Ped's translation, but he said her words literally meant that they treated it as sacred – and at other times they did not take it seriously enough. Two others told me of proposals they had made or opposed; Puy, who was thirteen, had proposed that all the rules that were no longer applied should be discarded, but had not carried her point; Duan, about the same age, had successfully opposed a staff motion that some of the dogs on the campus should be removed because they had no owners – she asserted that all the dogs had owners. Both transactions illustrate the children's confidence in their right to assert their own opinions. In no conventional school would a child dare to suggest that many of the rules were no longer applicable, let alone that such rules should be discarded. Duan won her point by her straightforward contradiction of an adult assertion; her view was accepted by the majority of the meeting.

I asked Rajani, the principal, how much she decided herself, how much the staff decided and how much the council decided. She said she had a sixth of the say, and the rest belonged to the teachers and the children.

Her largest area of authority is in drafting the curriculum, but the teachers are responsible for how they carry it out. Teachers show her the outline of any activities they propose, and she says whether they should go ahead or not, because she sometimes thinks the proposals are inappropriate. Recently one of the teachers had proposed that he should teach Western dance, but when the project began Rajani talked with him and dissuaded him from doing it. She thought the consumerist, glamorous lifestyle implied by the dancing would be harmful.

Rajani also makes most of the decisions about the budget.

The council deals firstly with rules, and secondly with activities. There is also now a school administrative body. This administrative body is responsible for making proposals, but their proposals have to be endorsed in the council. Last year there had been a problem when the administrative committee proposed that the students should plant the rice shoots. What happened was that many of the children did not know how to do rice-shoot planting properly, so they damaged too many rice shoots. After that it was agreed that all proposals would have to be endorsed by the council.

I asked to see a copy of the school rules, and it took a long time to find one. Ped translated them for me during our journey to Bangkok for our flight out. Several of them refer to the Justice Committee, and show that its responsibilities reach well beyond the enforcement of rules.

2.12   The Justice Committee shall be made up of one adult, two teenagers and two students of grades four to six.

2.2   The Justice Committee must inspect the houses at least twice a week.

2.3   Those who find lost items must bring them to the Justice Committee.

2.7   Abandoned blankets shall be held by the Justice Committee for five days. If the owners don't turn up, they go into the school store.

2.10   Poisonous snakes can be killed without permission from the Justice Committee.

6.9   Those who are fifteen and over are allowed to bathe at the river without seeking permission from the Justice Committee [so younger children must seek permission, presumably]

6.10   The Justice Committee is responsible for assigning someone to keep the school area clean.

The punishments that the Justice Committee can impose entail missing out on the daily sweets or the daily fruit, being grounded into a certain area, a simple warning, having to make an apology and occasionally a fine, but as the children have no money this fine usually has to be converted into public service or paid in sweets.

Other rules illustrate the wide variety of concerns in the community.

1.1   *Teenagers are not allowed to play or chat in the dark.*

1.4   *No gambling.*

1.6   *Those involved in bullying or soliciting others to bully or physically harm new children are subject to double the normal penalty.*

1.8   *No tree can be cut down. Penalty: replanting and caring for the new tree.*

2.9   *Those aged seven and under have the right not to attend the meeting.*

2.20   *Each dog must be owned by someone. If that dog causes damage the owner is responsible. If a dog bites, it must be removed from the school.*

5.3   *Drinking water must not be wasted, and cannot be used for washing your hands.*

6.4   *Only guitarists are allowed to have long fingernails.*

9.3   *You are not allowed to ring the bell for fun.*

9.13   *Harming animals or insects. Penalty: five days loss of rights [to sweets and fruit, but see rule 2.10 above].*

9.17   *If you fart in the meeting you lose your rights for one day.*

There are many more rules which deal mainly with administrative affairs, health and cleanliness, straightforward rules about food and play, and a few specific safety rules. My impression was that the community relied far more on common sense than on rules, and this impression was reinforced by the difficulty Ped had in finding a complete list. Several of the rules, such as the one about long fingernails and the one about not cutting down trees, seem more like responses to particular situations than necessary laws. We often saw children breaking a rule that said they had to wear shoes at all times, and I am told that the little boys who sang into my tape recorder were breaking the rule against obscene language, but these did nothing to interrupt the general atmosphere of friendliness and peace.

The profusion of rules seems at first to be difficult to reconcile with the sense of freedom in the school. The same contradiction exists at Summerhill and Sudbury Valley, two of the most famous of the older free schools anywhere in the world. There are various justifications offered: the rules are made by the children themselves, because they see them to be necessary; children like making rules; if there are no rules then order depends on authoritarian intervention by adults; rules give a sense of security, because everyone knows where they stand; adults can intervene in potentially harmful situations by relying on previously decided rules without have having to exert personal authority. Whatever the reason, there is no doubt that the children in these free schools who make this plethora of rules, nevertheless have a dignity and independence that is impossible in a school where rules have been imposed by adults.

I commented to Mikka at one point that I had not seen any child crying, and I had not seen any quarrels. (I did see two children crying later, and one brief quarrel.) She replied that of course there was occasional crying, particularly from certain children, and that the quarrels that arose were often dealt with by the older children, who were very good at it. She said, though, that all the staff had to lock their rooms, and recently there had been some money stolen. The culprit had been found, and turned out to be someone who had been at the school for quite a long time. Nothing much was made of it because it was agreed at a meeting that if you had learnt to steal when you were very young it was difficult not to take the opportunity when it cropped up.

It is worth noting that there is no rule against stealing. It is something everyone knows to be wrong, without reminding. Bullying, on the other hand, is the subject of several rules, in spite of the way the older children often deal with problems among the younger ones. Perhaps this is because it happens more often. There are very few incidents of theft in a year, and although the classrooms are kept locked up when not in use, the library is frequently open and apparently unattended. "The library is in fact attended to by staff," Ped told me. "Sometimes, my wife, who is in charge, asks a reliable adolescent boy to help look after it. Incidence of books taken away without permission does happen, but not at an alarming scale."

The children's point of view

The children I spoke to all emphasised their sense of freedom, and unless I asked them about the meetings they did not express any opinions about rules. Several of them had been terribly homesick when they first arrived – Mai said she had cried "for three days and three nights", which is a Thai expression for a very long time – but soon Moo Baan Dek became more of a home to them than their original homes. A ten-year-old boy called Dao told me that everyone was happy at Moo Baan Dek. Duan said the most important thing about the place was the love shown to the children, and she said that she herself loved everybody there. An eighteen-year-old called Boy, when I asked him what he thought of the younger children, cynically expecting him to say that they were sometimes a nuisance, replied that he thought the most important thing was that they should be happy. Mai talked about the way she took advantage of as many opportunities as possible, spending all her afternoons in the craft workshops, taking part in the performance groups and working enthusiastically in the gardens. She said that before she had arrived at the age of four she had been trained to be absolutely obedient, but she was not so obedient any more. The staff, she said, were not as warm as parents, more like brothers and sisters.

Puy told me she did not often go home because she was usually busy with the performance group, which put on productions, sometimes even in Bangkok, as a fund-raising exercise.

Mai is also in the performance group. They perform folk stories, their own stories, sometimes even political stories. In one of the latter the Burmese oil gas pipeline was represented as a dragon. A Bangkok company rents a venue for these performances, and an insurance company gives them a big hall once a year.

You can leave the school when you have finished elementary education, which may be at any age, as many of the children have been seriously held back by their previous experiences. Otherwise you may stay on at Moo Baan Dek and either go to the local secondary school, twenty kilometres away, or do vocational training in the school workshops or work experience elsewhere in the locality. You can also start work in Bangkok, living in a hostel run by the Foundation for Children. I spoke to two of the older students who had begun to move out from the school.

Boy had been at Moo Baan Dek for nine years, and was looking after the pottery workshop while the teacher was away. He had been offered payment, but he had refused it because he did not think he would be good enough at organising the children. He had made friends outside Moo Baan Dek when he went to the local secondary school, and thought they were just like his friends inside, except that they were able to smoke, drink and stay out late. He did not seem particularly envious, because he had had three advantages at Moo Baan Dek – the opportunity to learn to play the guitar, to play sport, and to meditate. Boy is now studying in the English Department in the Faculty of Humanities, Ramkamheang University.

Namwaan was sixteen, and had been going to the secondary school for four years. The children have to leave in the Moo Baan Dek bus at seven o'clock in the morning, and they come back by public transport around five or six in the evening. I asked her about the differences she saw between Moo Baan Dek and the conventional school.

Namwaan: *Here there is more freedom. I can do many things for myself, for example at the school I am forced to conform to rules, I have to dress the way they like, but here you can do whatever you like.*
DG: *Are your friends at school just like your friends used to be here?*

Namwaan: *My friends outside can't settle problems among themselves because they use force against each other more than using reasons, but we find that people here use reasons and talk problems over, and secondly I find people here have more intimate relationships. I feel closer to my friends here.*

DG: *And what about the teachers? Are they different?*

Namwaan: *Yes, very different. Teachers here do not just teach, they also take the parental roles, and I can bring my problems to the teachers here openly. But the teachers in my present school, I can take matters to them, but they will just refer them to, maybe, the administration of the school. And sometimes the problem will not be solved.*

DG: *What about the lessons themselves? Are you learning interesting things at the new school?*

Namwaan: *It is good that we get to know new friends, and we get to know the outside world. That helps us. We gain new experience about what is going on outside Moo Baan Dek.*

DG: *Would you have liked it if you could have done the same courses at Moo Baan Dek, or are you pleased to have gone out?*

Namwaan: *The school is too tightly disciplined. Even my friends who have only been to state schools, they complain too that they don't like the system, it is too rigid, too regimented, and they would like to have freedom to act on their own.*

DG: *Would you be able to learn as much of what is necessary for your exams if it was freer at that school?*

Namwaan: *I can learn anywhere.*

DG: *Is there anything like a school council at your new school?*

Namwaan: *There is a student committee, but the student committee has no real power. They work according to the orders sent down from the teachers, and their work is just to see that the students conform to the rules, and that they dress properly, and all that. It is not like Moo Baan Dek, where in the council the students and teachers take part equally, and students sometimes overrule adults. We can manage adults in many ways, here.*

DG: *When you first went to your present school was it difficult to cope with the work which you had to do?*

Namwaan: *It was difficult to adjust at first, and I was a little bit scared because I had no friends there and had to make new ones. And here I could decide whether to attend class or not. Sometimes I used to make plans with friends and we just missed a class and went somewhere else to do something more exciting.*

DG: *What are you going to do when you leave school?*

Namwaan: *I very much want to do something with computers.*

DG: *Do you learn computer studies at your new school?*

Namwaan: *Very little. It's very basic. I learnt most of what I know here at Moo Baan Dek.*

DG: *What is the part of Moo Baan Dek that you miss most?*

In the computer room

Namwaan: *Freedom. They don't have freedom there. I think that if children want to do anything at all that is not harmful to society or to other people they should be allowed to do it.*

DG: *Does it feel like your home here? Rather than any other place in the world?*

Namwaan: *I am more at home here. I have a strong bond with this place because I have lived here longer than in my home town. I was from the north. Even though I like my home town, I feel a stronger bond with this place, because here I made new friends, I met new people, I had different experiences, and most important of all, I grew up here.*

DG: *Are there people here you think of as your parents, or do you not need to have parents?*

Namwaan: *Rajani. And there is Pibhop. They are both kind of parents. I feel very close to them, they are the people I feel closest to here. Not many of the other adults stay very long, and some of them leave because they can't stand the students. I don't feel that intimate with them.*

And after Moo Baan Dek?

A good proportion of ex-students go on to university, but the jobs listed in the school brochure are farmer, sales person, driver, security officer, hospital staff, furniture-maker, mechanic and secretary. About ten of the twenty-seven staff at the school were ex-students.

This is how Rajani summed up the situation when I asked her about it:

Students used to have to leave when they were eighteen years old but now we have extended it to twenty years of age, in consideration of the retardedness in some of the children. These are the figures of the ex-students as far as we can track them down: eighteen of them work in business companies, three became temporary workers in some governmental offices, nineteen work in non-profit organisations, twenty-three are self-employed, as farmers and so on, and twenty-four of them work as wage labour. Four of them left to become street children again, but they didn't stay until they were that old. They left early.

A reminder

Let me describe a few more incidents that I observed.

After lunch one day I saw a dozen small boys clustered round another, aged perhaps ten, who was telling them a story. They were enthralled. They sat with their eyes fixed on him, in absolute silence except when he led them into laughter. His story lasted the best part of half an hour.

Four little boys were playing on a pile of straw near our guest house, when a teenager appeared. The straw was evidently being set aside for some purpose, and should not have been jumped on. The little boys fled, the teenager called them back, and one of them came. A group of girls joined the teenager and together they talked to the culprit. He looked contrite, and waited a little while by himself before walking after his friends who had escaped. Apart from the calling back of the boys as they were running off, there had been no raised voices. There was no adult anywhere near.

When I was testing my tape recorder and allowing some boys to sing into it, the microphone was soon firmly in the hands of a dominant group. Some younger children climbed onto the table and were obviously longing for a turn, so I pointed them out to the other boys, and they allowed them a turn without question. When I finally decided it was time to pack away the microphone because the little ones were not treating it carefully enough, the big boys helped me to do so.

Although there was occasional naughtiness, the atmosphere was so contented, and the children, even the very youngest, seemed so independent, so purposeful, so helpful and so friendly that Lynette and I completely forgot why we had come to see the place, and why the children were there. We just enjoyed ourselves.

I was reminded when Ped told me of the background of some of the children I had interviewed.

Dao was the son of a Burmese rebel, whose parents had both been killed. He was left with a monk, who beat him regularly.

Boy did not know his parents. His birth had never been registered, and he was one of the children whose existence had only been officially recognised after long efforts by Moo Baan Dek.

Puy came from the slum at the Klongtoey port in Bangkok. She had been adopted by another charitable foundation, where she was sexually abused, so her aunt brought her to Moo Baan Dek. Both her parents were in gaol for drug-trafficking.

Duan's parents each had a new partner. Her mother brought her to Moo Baan Dek because she was being abused by her step-grandfather, who had probably also abused her elder sister. She could go home from time to time, because her family lives in a nearby slum, but the school does not like her to go because of the danger of abuse.

Mai had been living with a mad aunt in a bamboo shed, with nothing to eat. Her mother now visits once in a while, each time with a new husband.

I asked Mikka whether she usually remembered the children's backgrounds. This is her reply.

Sometimes I am aware, but in everyday life I don't think about it a lot because I live with the children and play with them a lot and they are my friends too, and I could if I wanted ask them about their background but that would seem bad for the children and for our relationship. I don't treat them differently because I know what they come from. Sometimes I feel sorry for them, when I compare their life to my own life. I had a father and mother and everything, you know, but here they have a lot of friends and a lot of people who care about them. They take care of each other really well. So in everyday life I don't, but sometimes, yes.

When I looked at our photographs, after we had come back to England, I saw that some of them looked like the kind of photographs you see in the National Geographic Magazine, taken by anthropologists or explorers. It was a great surprise, because we had not felt like anthropologists or explorers, but like friends among friends. The atmosphere at Moo Baan Dek is so powerful that even white-skinned people from a country halfway round the world can immediately feel at home. And we felt welcomed by children who came from lives of misery and poverty and pain.

At the beginning of this account I quoted the statistic about the 150 children at Moo Baan Dek in 1999 who were classified by reasons of intake. I repeat the figures here:

Abuse	*29*
Abandonment	*25*
Broken home	*54*
Homelessness (runaway)	*16*
Orphanage	*26*

And they welcomed us as friends.

The Foundation for Children
(http://www.ffc.or.th)

Moo Baan Dek is only one of the projects run by the Foundation for Children. The objectives of the foundation are:

> *To provide opportunites for underprivileged and homeless children to fully develop their physical, intellectual and creative potentials.*
>
> *To see healthy alternatives in education and child-rearding in which the dignity of children is upheld and their opinions considered.*
>
> *To assist and cooperate with individuals and organisations working for children's education and welfare.*
>
> *To bridge the differences between children and older generations, so those children may be recognised and treatd as worthy and equal members of society.*
>
> *To protect children who are abused and negelected, and to restore their family relationships.*
>
> *To campaign for public awareness on children's rights.*

It runs more than twenty different projects, including:

> *FFC Publishing House*
> *Baan Tantawan Nutrition Centre*[1]
> *Food Development Program for Children and Communities*[2]
> *The Promotion of the Elders' Roles in Child and Community Development*
> *Eye Health Care for Children in Community*
> *Youth Development Centre: School-Factory Project*[3]
> *The Rural Library Project*
> *Sports for Youth and Community Project*
> *Daycare Centres for Child Development*
> *Basic Necessities for Community*[4] *(Helping communities to become self-sufficient by supporting them in income-generating supplementary occupations.)*

1   This is a shelter for malnourished children, which developed to create children's centres in slum communities. These were later taken over by the communities themselves.

2   A scheme which started by enabling poor children to go to school by paying for their lunches, and developed into encouraging local communities to cultivate their own food.

3   Vocational courses within the children's own home towns.

4   Helping communities to become self-sufficient by supporting them in income-generating supplementary occupations.

Butterflies, Delhi

The background

The children associated with Butterflies are street and working children in the city of Delhi. They are not only poor, underprivileged and working to survive, but also often deliberately hindered, by the adults around them, from acquiring any sort of schooling at all. Some live in slums, or *bastis*, where families, often large families, crowd into single-room shelters made of bamboo and bits of old plastic sheeting. Many of these children do go to school, but others are forced to work by their parents, and are beaten if they come back in the evening without enough money.

The majority live actually in the streets and have a degree of freedom, in that when they have earned enough money for the day they can spend the rest of the time as they please, although those who have jobs with stall-keepers or in restaurants may be forced to work for fourteen, fifteen or some say even eighteen hours a day. The commonest job is rag-picking, which means collecting litter from the streets into sacks, and taking it to recycling firms who will buy it. Other children work as shoe-cleaners or as porters at the railway station or the bus station, or help at market stalls. Garages also sometimes take them on as cheap labour. They earn about thirty rupees a day, that is to say fifty English pence – a sum that in England would buy you a small loaf of bread. In Delhi it is enough to buy the day's cheap food and perhaps a place in a night shelter.

If you do not work you go hungry.

In 1995/1996 the Butterflies children made their own report on street life. It discussed three problems: the police, education and recreation. The violence of the police towards children is extremely shocking, and occasional references to it will occur later in this account, but my central concern is education. Here are some of the comments that the young researchers collected, quoted from the report:

Education is the biggest thing in the world. By studying we can make our futures. We can become lawyers, policemen or politicians. While traveling by train, we can talk to the T. T. [train ticket inspector], we can get good jobs, earn respect, write letters, read bus numbers, do calculations and not be cheated. We all have the right to education, but when do we get to study?

Education is very important because when other people sign and we make thumb impressions, we feel very ashamed. If we study, no one will call us "Angoota Chap" (thumb impressionist).

Some children cannot study when their parents die. I used to go to school but when my father died I left school because my chacha-chacha [uncle] did not let me study.

We do not have any money at home. Papa is very old. My younger brother and sister have their expenses as well, so I pick rags. I do not know where the government school is. It is not in our jhuggi-jhopri basti.

My father is an alcoholic. He does not work. My mother washes dishes in people's homes and saves money. She tells me to study. But I feel pity. I share the work at home and pick rubbish. All the money gets spent on rations and water. How can I go to school?

They should think about our homes first – and why we left home and live on the streets. Forget about education – if we study we will all die hungry. Parents, brothers, sisters, will all die. The Government cannot bring back our parents. If there is enough money for our homes to run, we would not run away from home, would not be forced to work but would have studied. We would like to study, but who will do all this?

When Butterflies conducted research into their own programme, one of the questions they asked was, "How do parents/communities hinder in your studies?" These were some of the answers:

There is hardly anybody who wants us to study.
The kabadiwala [buyer of rags] complains to our parents if we don't collect enough rags.
The smakias [drug-dealers] do not like us going and studying.
When there are liquor shops around.

The liquor shop problem is two-sided. It is not only that the children can buy alcohol themselves; much more important is that their fathers can buy alcohol. On another occasion when street children were asked to identify their problems, drunkenness in adults and the consequent beatings came up at the top of the list with police violence.

Nevertheless, children can and do buy their own alcohol, but it is not only drinking that may tempt them. There is also smoking, ganja, smack, charas, sniffing correcting fluid, gambling and lotteries.

Drug-dealers encourage them to steal. And both inside and outside their homes they are always in danger of sexual abuse, sometimes leading to hospitalisation.

When Butterflies tried to encourage children to save money by offering them one hundred per cent interest on any money they saved for a year, they turned down the offer, because they did not know whether they would still be alive after so long.

Our Introduction to Butterflies

Rita Panicker, the founder of Butterflies, Ishani Sen, one of the street educators, and Amin, a fourteen-year-old street child from the programme, came to the 2000 IDEC (International Democratic Education Conference) in Tokyo, which was where Lynette and I met them. Amin spoke at one of the workshops. This is some of what he said:

My name is Amin. I have come on behalf of the Child Workers' Union, from the capital of India, that is Delhi. I want to speak on behalf of the child workers in Delhi, and I want to start more particularly about the street children in Delhi. Children come on the streets because of various reasons. Some because of the conflict in the family. Families break down, and that's why they come, and some come because they don't have enough work. We work hard on the streets, but in spite of that we face a lot of problems. We are harassed by the police, we need to look for space in the night to sleep on the street, and there are times when people, the general public, really look down upon us and the police are blaming us for crimes we have not committed.

In this situation education is the last thing we have in mind. But there are organisations who are working with us and they really think of different ways of involving us and getting us into the education system.

Organisations like Butterflies play a great role. They have given us our freedom to play, we can go to them and just play, we can just keep making drawings, we go to the children's council meetings and that's where participation becomes important. In the council meetings we can express our opinions, we can say what we want to learn.

In our union we discuss various problems of child workers; for example, there is a government-run Observation Home, where children stay, and there a child was beaten very badly, and the case was hushed up, it was not disclosed to the public, and then we got to know. The Union went up to the government to restart this case and to disclose all the information to the public.

Another example of what we have done. Very recently, that's one and a half years back, in our country there was a war with Pakistan, and in the place called Kargil that was where the war was taking place, and lots of people were dying, but the most affected population were the children of both the places in the villages, and in the union we discussed about it and we thought that it was important that we should be with the children of that area who were getting affected by the war and we collected money to send it to the children of both the countries.

...

I feel education is not only for academic education, it is education for life. And that is what we believe in, and that's why our education includes things like Juvenile Justice Act and Child Rights and United Nations Convention for the Rights of the Child because unless we have information we will not be able to fight for our rights.

...

We act for child's rights two different ways. We have a wallpaper, a newspaper, where we write about our conditions, what we do and the problems we face and that is a media of the Child's Union, to reach to the other people, the adults of the society. We also have a theatre group where we take up issues like what happens to children who are working in restaurants, what is happening to child labourers and look at children in different parts of the city.

From time to time as a part of the work of the group we have rallies [protests], like last year there were a lot of children who were taken off the street and put into remand homes for no reason, and we decided to have a rally. And on the 10th of December, which is a human rights day we took out a rally advocating the cause, and we went to meet the chairman of the national human rights commission, and gave a petition to him, stating that we are working children, and not a burden and we have every right to be treated as human beings.

...

In our country when legislations are made there is no participation of children. Even when legislation is related to children there is no participation whatsoever, not only from the child labourers, no children can participate in the decision-making, so I have a request to IDEC and to all of you, that if there is a pressure, an international pressure on different governments that when legislation is made about children, children should be able to participate, and if there is a kind of consensus about it you can write letters to different governments and that would be a step forward to children's participation.

There is a kind of brotherhood, there is a kind of comradeship among us, and we are all part of the society so when we help each other and we discuss our problems that makes us much more concerned for the collective problem of the society.

There was a question about where he got the confidence to stand up in front of a large group of adults and talk about his problems, and another about what he would do if someone offered him a thousand dollars.

I live on the street, and by living on the street I get the confidence. But you must remember that when first a child comes on the street, he doesn't – he is not able, he is not that powerful, he will not be able to speak in that way, but once he starts living on the street he starts fighting for his life, fighting for his survival, that gives him the power. And that is education for him, to be able to speak for himself. And when you talk of money, I am a working child and I value my labour. Even if you were to give me a lot of money I would not take it. I am proud of the work I am doing.

After this workshop I went to talk to Amin and the two Butterflies adults and asked whether they would allow me to interview them. They agreed, and first I asked Rita about the very beginning of the scheme. She started by telling me about her experiences in Bombay, before she came to Delhi.

I used to go to work regularly by train, about two hours, two hours going and two hours coming, and invariably in the trains I would meet children and they always fascinated me because they looked so exciting, they would have such a good rapport with their own companions, chatting away, playing away, and although looking at them you knew they must be leading very hard lives, there was such a positive look on their faces. Well, I used to strike conversations with them whenever I had an opportunity, and they used to tell me all these stories. Now I know that they were all wild stories – some of them seemed just like screen scripts for the Hindi popular cinemas. But I really used to engage them in conversations and discussions and got very much interested in their lives.

And once an eighteen-year-old boy came up to my husband and tapped him and said, "Brother do you remember me?" He looked at him and in a minute he said, "Aren't you Vardarajan?" and the boy said, "Yes." My husband said, "What are you doing? Where are you?" and the boy said, "Back from where you picked me up." And Gerry was totally shocked. And I was surprised and curious because until then I didn't know that my husband Gerry had been with street children many years ago. And now I heard that he had picked up this guy when he was eight years old from the Bombay Central Railway Station, and that this child was saying that he was now back on the streets. It was kind of a curiosity to me, whereas for my husband it was a major shock.

We invited him home for dinner, and he came, and then he came in every Sunday. Gerry and I would really discuss with him what had gone wrong, what had happened. And one thing that he told me that struck me very much was that he said, "I got protection from the street when I was taken into this institution, yes, I had a bed to sleep, I had shelter, yes, they gave me an education, they gave me a technical education but at the age of eighteen I had to leave. That's when I realised that that was my home, and that I had to

*learn again to live in society, to be a part of the mainstream, and I had lost all
my survival skills."*

*Then he told me that there were quite a few of his companions in the same
situation. We started meeting with his companions also. They started coming
every Sunday for a meal, in fact they used to cook the dinner and we used to
have discussions, and I realised that all of them had a high school diploma,
all of them had some kind of a technical education, but they were very
disillusioned and frustrated young men. I could just imagine the
disillusionment and the frustration that must have gone in their brains
because for about ten years they had been in an enclosed protected
environment, and now they were back on the streets, and with all the
education and the technical training in their heads, and they found it very
difficult to accept their situation. And there were moments when they were so
frustrated some of them were even thinking of suicide, not wanting to live any
more. So we had these discussions and then I asked them, "How about coming
together and forming a cooperative? You could first form a credit union. All
of you have an ad hoc job, so if you can put money into a bank and build up
capital, then you can get a loan and you can go to any of the housing
cooperatives and tell them that, look, you are carpenters, masons, electricians,
plumbers, and that you will take over the maintenance of the building, and as
a cooperative you will really get business going." They liked that idea, and we
started like that.*

*But when I started, David, I was not thinking of an organisation, I was just
doing it out of my interest and from the heart. I wanted to help them, so I just
did it as an individual. But about two or three months later my husband got
transferred to Delhi and I had to go too, so then I would travel from Delhi to
Bombay every month, but it never worked. Anyway, it died. And till today I
cannot forgive myself for having done that and not brought it to a logical
conclusion, the system should have been put in place so they could carry on the
work. I gave them an idea, showed them the way, but then I just left, so I felt
very bad about it.*

*So then in Delhi I decided that I would work with children. I decided not to
go back to academics and not to join a university and take up lecturing again,
and I started walking the streets of Delhi, first by myself, getting to know the
children, speaking to them, getting ideas from them. And then another person
joined me and slowly the project began, but I was also very clear in my mind
that I didn't want to start an organisation just for the sake of establishing a
voluntary organisation. I felt that one needs to know very clearly in one's mind
what is the goal and objectives of having an organisation, and what should be
the philosophy and the principles on which this organisation should be based.*

*I spent about six months travelling around the country, visiting various
innovative projects for street children, I spoke to their founders, met the
children and the educators, and learnt a lot from them. When I came back I
would not have to make the same mistakes as they had made. At the same time
I was also keenly observing their approaches, working with children, and I*

knew that some of the things which they were doing, I wouldn't do. And one of them was that they were not very democratically run, these organisations. Children participated but they participated as beneficiaries, as recipients. There was no concept of being an active participant. And that's why I felt that our organisation should be democratic.

I asked what role she took in the organisation now.

Now I have a lot of administration to do and it takes a lot of my time, more so because one has to raise funds. Apart from that my time also goes for various meetings, and planning, and I also take time off in training. Whatever time I can squeeze out I also do research work and writing, but I make it a point to meet children. They have their monthly meetings, their children's council meetings, and they let me know the date and the venue way ahead of time, and I always go to them, because that's one thing that I don't want to miss out on. Then we have an advisory committee meeting which meets with me. There are about eleven, twelve children who come to this meeting. They tell me exactly what they think about what's happening, and what they don't like. I bounce off ideas for them to see is it relevant, do they find it useful or not, which is very good, and children have free access to me any time. They have my telephone numbers and my secretary knows that any time a child calls there is no question of anything – it just gets transferred. They can come – my door is always open. Any time they can walk in. But going every day to the field is something I am unable to do.

...
Participation is a difficult thing to understand, accept and act upon because each one of us has been socialised in different ways. I was socialised to respect age and accept whatever is told to me by an older person. Elders never consulted us children on anything; they tell us of their decisions. However, I was always uncomfortable with this hierarchical relationship. Therefore, I would often question, sometimes disagree with the decisions of my elders and it was seen as being rude and impolite. But, I knew I had the right. My various experiences in life have given me the courage to speak my mind and to value democratic principles. It was a struggle then and continues to be one now, which one has to recognise. Today, every day I have to ask myself, "Did I consult the children? Did I listen to what they were saying? Or did I just hear a little bit and then make my own decisions?"

In a written description of Butterflies Rita has told how the adults first learnt to listen properly.

In the first year of our work, although we spoke and discussed about children having a right to freedom of expression when it came to the crux we somehow forgot about it or perhaps did not take it seriously, until it was brought home to us by the children. It happened in October 1987. As a team we were barely five persons. Diwali festival was approaching and generally there was a festive look and atmosphere in the city. The street educators decided that we must celebrate Diwali by gathering all children at Central Park in the heart of the city, have fireworks and a feast of sweets. Street educators called a meeting of children and having decided the activity they informed all the children about their decision and asked for their approval. In Butterflies nothing is given free, children contribute for everything. Therefore a group of children questioned the decision of the street educators of wanting to celebrate Diwali by fire crackers and sweets; according to them it was a waste of money. They told the street educators they would rather save that money to buy sweaters and woollen clothes as winter was fast approaching rather than waste it on fire crackers. Their decision prevailed.

This incident is what gave birth to the concept of Bal Sabha (Children's Council). It has proved to be the single most important key to sustain and develop children's participation, thereby empowering them.

Lynette and I felt we must learn more about this astonishing organisation, and asked permission to visit them in Delhi. We were invited to spend a week there in January 2001.

First day in Delhi

In January in Delhi it is still cold. We were staying in the Gandhi Peace Foundation, where we luckily had a room with three beds. This meant that we had an extra ration of blankets to share, but in spite of that we still went to bed in all our clothes.

On our first morning we drove off in a taxi to the Butterflies office in New Delhi, where we were welcomed by Ishani and another Butterflies worker, a young Welshwoman called Claire O'Kaine, and later had a chance to talk to Rita as well. The office has perhaps four small rooms and one slightly larger one with a table with eight or ten chairs round it, where we sat and talked. About thirty staff are organised from this centre.

At the time we visited, Butterflies had eight contact points where street educators would meet children at mutually agreed times every day. These were at Jama Masjid, Kashmiri Gate, Fateh Puri, Peti Market, Chandni Chowk and the Inter-State Bus Terminal (ISBT) in Old Delhi, and at Connaught Place and New Delhi Railway station in New Delhi. There are two educators to each contact point. The contact points are in places where many children gather to earn money – near the markets, at the stations and, in the case of Connaught Place, in a tourist area.

Claire had some drawings that a group of children had made. They had been asked to draw a boy and a girl, and to say what the advantages and disadvantages of being a boy or a girl were. All but two out of a group of about twenty thought it was better to be a boy. Most of the children who come to Butterflies have never held a pencil; they love to draw, but start like the very young, drawing people with their arms coming out of their heads. One such drawing of a girl had a man or boy beside her with a stick in his hand; he was apparently beating her, as she was crying and had red marks on her.

Some of the children who come to the contact points do not want to study, because they would rather just attend health instruction or Bal Sabha or drama, or just draw or play. When they are fourteen or fifteen they will wish they had learnt to read and write and will very much regret not having done so. Street educators try to point this out to the younger ones, in groups, individually and sometimes at the Bal Sabha. It does not always work, but there are many who spend two or three hours a day working with Butterflies.

Rita emphasised that literacy and education are not the same. In one sense the children are highly educated – they know how to survive, and are in some ways much more mature than their coevals. For this reason the curriculum that is offered cannot be childish, and special materials have to be developed. People tell her that the children must be rehabilitated. "Rehabilitated to what?" she asks. To the mainstream, they tell her, but in her view the street children are already in the mainstream, closer to the mainstream than children who have to stay in schools.

Both Ishani and Claire told us that the children had extremely good memories; when you cannot write anything down, you have to remember it, and your memory develops. Claire said the non-formal education practised by Butterflies helped children to analyse and question and to find out information for themselves; formal education often kills these abilities.

I asked Rita what she considered to be success, and she started with the fundamentals. Success, she said, is when the children trust the adults. Only then do other things follow. It is success when children learn to read and write, even though they may get no academic qualifications; it is success when they succeed in personal projects, such as research, or finding a solution to a problem. And of course it is a success if they go on to high school and get good jobs. Four from this last category, who, according to Rita, had been very strong and difficult personalities, are now working for Butterflies.

After our meeting in the office, Ishani took us out to visit two of the contact point areas. The first one was Delhi railway station. Children come there because there is work carrying bags and cleaning the trains, sweeping under the seats and collecting rubbish and bottles, it is the first place they come to when they arrive in Delhi, there are places to buy food, there is water available, it is easy to hide in the crowd, and there is a place to sleep. The place to sleep is on the roof. There was a child sleeping there under a single blanket when we crossed the footbridge. We had been cold sleeping fully dressed, under three blankets, indoors.

Butterflies has chosen the station as a contact point because there are at least two hundred children there, and the new arrivals from all over the country are in danger. The educators are there from ten in the morning until one in the afternoon each day, because at that time there are fewer long-distance trains, and therefore there is less work.

Ishani stopped to talk to two boys who appeared to be about ten years old. They were smiling and friendly, and waved goodbye to us when we walked on. Ishani told us that when the street educators meet such people, formal education is not the priority. The priority is to make each child feel trusted, secure and precious. Only then can formal learning take place. When the children are frequently driven away by the adult porters and attacked by the police without provocation, it is astonishing that this trust can be established. Perhaps it is helped by the fact that sometimes, when they try to intervene, the Butterflies adults get beaten by the police as well.

Ishani told us of an occasion early in her time with Butterflies when she had seen a child being beaten by a man on the fringes of an insalubrious park, and had wanted to intervene. She was stopped by one of the Butterflies boys, who said, "You must not go there. They are all pimps. They will insult you even though you are a teacher. We will deal with that." This made her ask herself the question, "Who is the protector?" She told us she had learnt two lessons from this experience, firstly that she must be careful, and secondly that she had to learn from the children as well as teach them.

As we walked on round the railway station we passed several policemen. They all carried bamboo poles, four to six feet long, of varying thickness. Ishani told us of one boy who was being chased by the police and had hidden by dropping over the edge of the bridge and hanging onto the rail with his hands. A policeman beat his knuckles until he fell and injured his back. Butterflies took the policeman to court, but the justice system was so slow that in the end the child asked for the case to be dropped.

Our next visit was to Connaught Place, the circular park in the middle of the New Delhi tourist district. The work opportunities for children there include shoe-polishing, selling balloons and garlands, working in small garages and of course rag-picking; here there is plenty of rubbish thrown out of shops that they can collect and sell. There are other attractions, too. The Hanuman temple gives out free food, and there are other food shops around. Tourists pay more for shoe-cleaning, so the boys can charge five rupees rather than the usual three. When the children have earned a little money there are shops to go to, several cinemas and some video games arcades. Drugs are always available, provided by paedophiles in exchange for sex, or by drug-dealers aiming to build up a market.

Here the street educators work from two until five-thirty, because the mornings and the evenings are busy. Other people always gather round to see what is going on, and to ask the educators why they are bothering with these worthless urchins who will never make any use of what they are being taught. The educators simply ignore these questions, but the children often try to drive the audience away, asking whether they think they are animals in a zoo. The children are not allowed to sleep in the park at night, so they have to sleep in nearby alleys.

We ourselves met no children there, because they had all gone out on a picnic with their street educators. Butterflies had originally planned that we should spend the afternoon with the drama group, but the previous night one of the principal actors had been sodomised and was now in hospital.

A workshop run by children

The next day we were invited to attend a workshop on participation, run by our friend from Tokyo, Amin, aged sixteen, and Anuj, aged fourteen and also living on the streets.

It was held at the Kashmiri Gate contact point, one of the few where some privacy is possible. St. James' Church has allowed Butterflies to use its churchyard, a wide lawn surrounded by big trees, where there is also a water supply and lavatories.

We arrived early, and while we waited for the children to arrive I spoke to Dr. Pradeep, who runs the Butterflies Health Centre. Medical services are available for the children in a bus, which drives around from one contact point to another. I asked him what problems he had to deal with, and the ones that occurred to him first were skin diseases, both fungal and bacterial, respiratory problems due to pollution and smoking, hepatitis B, gonorrhoea, syphilis and other sexually transmitted diseases. No girl is safe on the streets, he said; the only possible career for them is prostitution. I asked him whether he was not in despair, and he replied that despair was not an option. There is a problem which exists and you have to face it and do what you can to cope with it. It is not possible to turn your back on it.

Amin and Anuj had participated in a ten-day regional workshop organised by Save the Children on "Training of Facilitators on Children, Citizenship and Governance". Children and adult facilitators from across Central and South Asia had taken part, and Amin and Anuj had been part of the planning team. After the workshop they were keen to share what they had learnt with other members of Butterflies. They brought up the subject at a monthly Bal Sabha, and it was agreed that they should run a one-day workshop on "Participation and Active Citizenship". They had to prepare a precise budget, which came to 2000 rupees, half of which was to be paid by Butterflies, and the other half raised from the children themselves, through their Bal Mazdoor Union, which is a trade union for street and working children for which they have not yet won official recognition. The workshop was attended by about thirty children, a dozen staff from Butterflies, Lynette and me.

We started sitting in a big circle. The boys explained what they were going to do and asked each of us to introduce ourselves. We heard that nearly all the children there were rag-pickers.

The first activity was a game for which we were divided into three teams. The teams had to stand in lines, and there were three competitions. The first was to make the line as short as possible, the second was to make it as long as possible while still touching each other, and the third was to make it as long as possible using anything else we could find to extend the line. What impressed me as a visitor was that Lynette and I, white-skinned, grey-haired and in my case elderly, were accepted into these games, which involved a lot of physical contact, without any doubt or self-consciousness.

At the end of the game the teams were asked to sit and discuss with each other the reasons why they had won or lost in the different competitions, and what they had learnt from them. Then we made a circle again and reported our findings.

Because the workshop was to last a full day, Amin and Anuj had had to organise food and refreshments as well as other activities, and there was now a tea break. We were joined by a group of girls from Kidwai Nagar, one of the slums where Butterflies works with children who are living with their parents. Dr. Pradeep had explained to me that there are very few girls actually living on the streets, because it is too dangerous for them. I realised that up to that time all the child participants in the workshop had been boys.

Before lunch we were redivided into six groups, the adults all in one group and the children in the other five. We were asked to discuss what we thought participation meant, why it was important, and how it could be promoted. Then we were to do plays or some other form of presentation to show our conclusions. The few girls were at first reluctant to separate and join different groups of boys, but they did so and played important parts in the performances. Amin and Anuj walked from one group to another to see how things were going, and commented that the adults were doing nothing but discussing, while the children were getting on with their plays. Nevertheless each group of children had appointed a scribe who wrote down their ideas.

After lunch Anuj and Amin divided the children into five groups and gave each group a written case study. They were to read these case studies and then show through drama how they could respond to them. The case studies reminded me that Rita had told us that the material given to the children could not be childish.

Case Study One: *You are a twelve-year-old boy. You live with your family which includes your mother, father and your fourteen-year-old sister. One day you find your sister crying as your parents have told her she has to get married. You also believe she is too young to get married. What can you do?*

Case Study Two: *You are a group of boys who are working in the railway station. One day you meet a girl who has run away from home. Someone has sexually abused her. You and your friends support the girl and go with her to file a case against the abuser, but the police do not want to file a case. What can you do?*

Case Study Three: *You are in a school, the teacher is often hitting children hard on the head. What can you do?*

Case Study Four: *Your friend works in a shop. One day his employer falsely accuses him of stealing and refuses to pay him his monthly wages. What can you do?*

Case Study Five: *You hear that one of your friends has been picked up by the police and placed in Dilli Gate Children's Home. What can you do?*

Lynette and I of course had to rely entirely on tone of voice and body language in our attempts to understand what was going on, but it was clear that the children's acting was good, and a number of stylised tricks, for instance a particular way of miming entrance through a door, showed that they were well used to this kind of work.

After these plays there was another break for tea, and a few of the younger children, who had begun to play around, were reluctant to come back for the final game. It was only then that I realised that we had all been together for five hours, and that Anuj and Amin had kept us concentrated and involved for all of that time. When the game itself was set, up everyone joined in enthusiastically again, but the boys were not able to hold people together well enough for a discussion afterwards, and the workshop closed.

The workshop discussions were all carefully recorded, and Butterflies has produced a full account of the proceedings.

There was no doubt that we had all learnt a great deal from our day, but there had been no lecturing or didactic teaching. Children and adults had talked together and learnt from each other. The level of discussion had been high: when the adults and children discussed participation separately the adults produced only ten points, whereas the children, admittedly in five groups, produced twenty-six; the adults were inclined to be general and abstract, whereas the children's points were more specific and practical.

As visitors we had learnt even more about Butterflies than we had learnt about participation. We saw how Amin and Anuj, supported by two Butterflies staff who nevertheless remained completely in the background, organised almost fifty people in a series of purposeful activities for almost six hours. We saw how the educators related to the children, as friends and colleagues rather than as authority figures, and that there was no hint of condescension. We saw how the street children worked together, enthusiastically and seriously, and we saw their laughter and enjoyment. We saw children capable of fluently taking down notes about what was being said. We saw a little of the deadly seriousness of some of the problems they have to face. We saw the girls welcomed into the group without question. We saw an event which cost the children themselves 1000 rupees, when they were each earning about 30 rupees a day, and we saw a dignity and purposefulness that were perhaps in part a result of not suffering the humiliation of being obliged to accept charity.

The Wall Newspaper

Two days later Lynette and I were invited to attend a meeting of the editorial board of the Butterflies wallpaper newspaper, *Bal Mazdoor ki Awaz* (*Voice of the Child Workers*). It was held in the meeting room at the Butterflies office. When we arrived at about ten o'clock, the board had already breakfasted and Ashfaq, one of the street educators, had given a lesson on the planets and the seasons, with a relevant poem.

About eight of the dozen editors and reporters were present, and their first job was to vote for a chair and a secretary. The chair was taken by a boy called Pappu, who we had already met elsewhere, and Anuj became secretary. The meeting was conducted in Hindi, but Ashfaq translated some of the discussions for us.

The agenda, written on the blackboard, was, "1. Girls (Javeed and Amin). 2. Report on workshop (Amin). 3. How could this meeting improve? (Amin)." The meeting was very orderly, governed effectively by Pappu, who overruled a proposal from Amin that Wazim, another boy who had befriended us, should be asked to leave because he was not taking it seriously. However, they already had enough material for the next two issues, and as publication is only every two months there was no pressing need to make more plans. The first agenda item was about how to make it possible for girls to contribute to the wallpaper, in spite of the fact that they were always being kept at work by their families. Various suggestions were made, and Ashfaq agreed to ask the street educators to bring them up at their contact point.

This arrangement between Ashfaq and the children who were running the meeting is characteristic of Butterflies. The children are responsible for what happens, but they often need the help and support of the educators. The names they give to the educators are Bhaiya and Didi – elder brother and elder sister – and that describes the relationship well.

The result of the wallpaper meetings is an A3 sheet which is published in Hindi and English. About five hundred copies are made. These are then posted in different places around the city. At the foot of the page stand the words:

Produced and Published by Street and Working Children.
The Editors and Reporters are children between the age of 9 and 16 years.

The style is direct, and the messages are powerful, as is shown by the following articles, which I quote also for their descriptions of the street children's problems in Delhi. These are the published English versions.

Filmi-Chat

In Delhi there are many video halls which shows films as cheap as Rs. 5/- for three films. Therefore lots of people go there to watch films. Children also go in large numbers. In old Delhi there are two main places – one is behind Rajghat in the slums near Power House and second is – slums of Peti Market near Red Fort. Among us street children these halls are known as Power House and Peti Market.

These video halls are very dirty and unclean. Here on the floor dirty and tattered mats are spread on which everyone sits and watch films. They show both Hindi and English films. Therefore lots of people go there to watch films especially those who live on the roads both adults and children. Though these video halls are open throughout the day, they are very crowded in the nights. This is because those who live on footpaths for them it is a problem where to spend nights, as a solution to this problem and simultaneously being entertained they buy a ticket of Rs. 5/- and enter these halls – watch a film till they want and then sleep in the hall itself. Here there are facilities of fans in summers and quilts in winters. It is really an interesting and good deal just in Rs. 5/- watch a film all night or sleep. It's both a hall and a night shelter.

But there is another reason for this crowd. Which is a cause of worry. It is that under the pretext of Hindi films they also show blue films. These X-rated films are not shown on fix times. They are shown in between the films for sometimes or generally in night after 2.00 a.m. or 3.00 a.m. for 30 to 35 minutes.

Most of the times children are sexually abused in these halls at Power House and Peti Market. At the hall, there are both adults and children therefore during blue films the grown ups get hold of the children for sex due to fear children do not object and even if they do and ask for help no one helps them including the owner of the hall. Sometimes children also willingly do with the adults. In winters this act is done easily under a sheet or a quilt in darkness no one knows who is doing what and also due to winters it is more crowded.

Didi and Bhaiya of Butterflies have many times talked about these wrong deeds to the police, but it was of no help. If a strict police officer comes, the halls are closed for some days but then they are again started. Due to this it seems that hall owners and police have a good understanding that's why police remains silent and police do not punish such people.

In these halls children's shoes and chappals also get stolen. Sometimes their pockets are picked and other times their money is snatched forcefully. We think the government should close such video halls and punish those who abuse children.

What does society think about street and working children?

On this issue we talked to many people, some in reply to our question gave us slaps and abuses and some talked to us properly. Here we are presenting the main excerpts from the talk:

When Raju asked an old man sitting in a 'Kabadi Wala' shop he abused him and said "you are a tapori [vagabond]" and while slapping him asked him to get lost.

When Suraj asked the owner of a video game parlour "what do you think about street children who come to play here". He said "they are nice they work hard to earn I only get angry on them when they fight with each other, make noise and sometimes even break my glasses. Then I scold and beat them."

When Pinto asked a shop keeper near Hanuman Temple "What do you think about street children?". He said "They are all beggars, when they work in my shop then I treat them as my servants, when they are picking rags on the streets in dirty condition then I think them to be thieves."

When Anuj and Anil talked to a policeman at ISBT he said "these children should be studying and going to school but due to poverty they have to pick rags. Sometimes children steal and if police does not beat them those people think that police are one with these children. Though our law book and our officers say that children should not be beaten but we are forced to beat them."

Anuj asked him "why some policemen snatch children's money" The policeman said "It is not this way the fact is when children are gambling then some police men and elders snatch the money. We only take money of children who gamble and then distribute this money among younger children" When Anuj asked him why they take 'hafta' [bribes] from children he said "we do not take 'hafta' from children, we take it from those grown ups or children who use footpath to spread their rags and scraps and buy this stuff".

When Anuj asked a "Kabadi Wala" what he thought of us. He said "those children who work hard to earn their living are good but those who pick pocket, I consider them bad."

When Parvez asked a "Dhaba [food stall] Owner" his opinion on children like us he said "I think they are nice but I want that the way they work hard for earning same way they should work hard in studying and then one day try to become a big man. You should also get rid of all the bad habits like gambling, taking alcohol and drugs and abusing. If you want to become good you should leave this place, by staying here you will be ruined, continue to work hard and never steal.

At ISBT itself Anuj and Anil talked to a shopkeeper what he thought about street children he said "The moment I see them I get irritated, they trouble us, if chappals are lying they secretly put them in their sack and go away. After giving Rs. 1/- they ask for tea if they do not get it they abuse and then run away. That is why I do not think nicely about such children". Then Anuj asked him "why shopkeepers like you do not pay small children like us after employing us for work." On this he said "I no more employ small children because I had a bad experience. Last year during winters two children were trembling due to cold and they were hungry also. They asked me for food and also requested me 'uncle please hire us, we have no one at home except brother and his wife. He had beaten us and asked us to go away.' I felt bad for them. I gave them food and kept them for work. Next day uncle of those children came looking for them along with the police. When he saw them working he got angry on me and asked me to pay for expenses. When I did not give it, the uncle filed a case against me and I was kept in a lock up for three days. I had to pay Rs. 20.000 for bail. I am still fighting the case. That is why I do not hire children nor feed them, may be again I would be caught for some unknown crime."

Each edition of the paper has room for two or three articles of this length, and a few shorter items. The children write them in Hindi, and they are translated for them by someone in the Butterflies office.

How do the Butterflies educators help an "angoota chap" who is ashamed at having to sign documents with his thumbprint to reach the stage of being able to write articles like these, and take coherent minutes at meetings? What we were able to learn about this during our short visit is the subject of my next section.

Non-Formal Education

We were not able to visit any of the contact points in completely public places, because our presence would have attracted too much attention from passers-by. However, we were able to go the contact points at Chandni Chowk and Jama Masjid, because the former is in the grounds of a Catholic girls' school, and the latter is in a night shelter.

A street educator's trunk

We went to Chandni Chowk with Ishani towards the end of one afternoon. The setting seemed ideal. There was a paved semi-circular terrace with a low wall round it where you could sit, overlooking a big, grassed play space. Against the back wall of the terrace was a big tin trunk which contained books and writing materials, posters and games. Ashfaq and Laxmi were there with perhaps twenty-five children, aged, at a guess, between six and thirteen. About half of them were girls. There were posters hanging on the back wall, one of them displaying the numbers from one to a hundred in rows of ten, and another showing a chart of fruit with their names in Hindi and English. Boys were writing out the numbers from one to a hundred on a blackboard, reading words from an alphabet poster, writing in exercise books. Five or six girls were sitting with Laxmi writing numbers on slates. Others were playing with large balls, running in the play space, practising diabolo, talking to Ashfaq. Ishani pointed out how the children were helping each other; the competitiveness of the outside world, she said, has no place here, because these children are used to living together in groups and depend on each other.

One boy invited me to play a card game with him, which we could do without speaking the same language, and a twelve-year-old boy called Javeed took me to the poster of numbers and taught me to count up to ten in Hindi. Then we went through the chart of fruits and another chart labelling parts of the body. He could read English letters perfectly.

It was remarkable how little disturbance we caused. Had we arrived in a classroom where all attention was focussed on the teacher, we would probably have interrupted the whole lesson. If the children had been working independently, but on tasks set by the teacher, they might well have seized the opportunity for a distraction. Here the children were doing whatever they wanted to do, and our arrival was interesting but not interesting enough to interrupt them. Those who were working were just as concentrated as those who were playing .

I looked in the tin trunk to see what was available. There were slates, exercise books, pencil cases, a basic arithmetic book; there were balls, diabolo, posters, cards with scenes from street life, alphabet playing cards, colouring materials; there were a few reading books, various board games, dice; there were children's drawings of houses, flags and people; there were plastic alphabets, flash cards and cards with words the children needed to recognise – POST OFFICE, EXIT and so on. There were also very carefully preserved savings books. (The children had no way of keeping their own money safely and so were used to spending it all as soon as they earned it. Butterflies' offer of one hundred per cent interest after a year had failed to persuade them to save, but most had been convinced by a new offer of one hundred per cent interest after six months.)

Practising writing numbers

Ishani helped us to speak to a twelve-year-old girl who told us that she couldn't go to school because her parents could not afford to pay for books and pencils, so she had been eager to come to Butterflies when she heard about it. She was learning to count and to read, and she preferred studying to playing. There were eight children in her family, five boys and three girls. The two other girls were both married, but the rest of them all worked picking rags until five o'clock in the evening and earned 15 to 25 rupees a day.

There was a little pile of rag-pickers' sacks on the terrace. They were large and dirty and made of coarsely woven plastic fibre; some were partly filled. When it was time to leave, their owners collected them, and in spite of the fact that we had of course already known intellectually that young children picked rags, it was a shock to see six- and seven-year-olds actually carrying off sacks as big as they were.

I looked at the picture cards that had been specially prepared by Butterflies to stimulate discussion. They showed children sleeping on the street, being accused of theft, being approached by strange men, sitting in the cinema, working in a garage, dreaming of a home in the country, being bullied – situations that were all too familiar. Formal teachers often try to avoid subjects that touch their pupils emotionally, because they feel that school is not the place for personal problems to be handled. The non-formal educators of Butterflies use subjects that do touch the children emotionally, because those are the subjects that children really want to talk and write about.

Ishani had come to the contact point to do some particular work with a group of girls. When she collected them together some of the smaller boys who were playing on the grass below came up to squeeze into the group and watch what was going on. Watching is a valuable way of learning.

Street girls are treated with even less consideration than street boys; they even have difficulty crossing roads, because cyclists and drivers will not slow down for them or try to avoid them. Ishani discussed this kind of situation with the girls, working with a big drawing of a girl on which were written the advantages and disadvantages of being a girl, as had been suggested on another occasion. She then divided them into two groups to make up plays, one about what happens to a girl at home, and the other about what happens to a girl in the street. It emerged that the girls at home also have problems – they are forced to do all the domestic work, they are married off when they are too young, they are beaten by their parents. The girls in the street are teased, and the men try to kiss them, even the shopkeepers they work for. Everywhere girls are looked down on. After the plays were performed, the girls stood in a ring and Ishani threw a ball to one after another of them; whoever had the ball had to suggest a solution to one of these problems.

The emphasis at the contact points differs according to the street educators who work there; at one there will be more story-books, at another more

Ishani (left) with a group of girls, and some boys eavesdropping

role-play and at another more art. At all the contact points there are occasional special activities, such as this role-playing for girls, or circus skills, or some special art project, but the trunk is always there too, and open, so that the children can choose to study if they want to. And many of the children do prefer to study, because – Ishani actually used the word "because" – no-one is obliging them to do anything.

Although the Chandni Chowk contact point is in the grounds of a private school, the gates are open, and while we were there two children who were not already members of Butterflies came and watched for a while. When they turned to go, Ishani hurried after them and persuaded one of them to come back and spend more time with the group.

The other contact point we visited was in the night shelter at Jama Masjid. The night shelter is a big room in a warehouse near the market. There are old rugs on the floor and a big pile of blankets in one corner. On the wall are a few scattered posters, including a copy of the *Bal Mazdoor ki Awaz*. There is also a stack of fifty lockers, where the children who use the night shelter regularly can keep their possessions. Amin showed me what he had in his locker – washing things, photographs stuck to the door, a cup, some spare clothes, a bottle of water and the remains of the box of chocolates we had brought for him, which he had been sharing with other children. There was hardly room for anything more. Javid showed Lynette what he kept in his locker; what particularly moved her was the needle and thread he kept to mend his clothes.

There were only eight boys in the room on the morning we visited, because it was cold, and the others were outside in the sun. On hot days there would be fifty there. The small number made it easy to see exactly what was going on. A tin trunk like the one we had seen at Chandni Chowk was open by the wall. Three boys were reading aloud to each other. One was on his own reading a comic. One was drawing. Amin was doing arithmetic. Another boy was writing, first squatting on the floor and then getting up to sit at the only table in the room. Javid was reading, somewhat hesitantly, with one of the two educators who were there.

In the trunk there were about thirty-five exercise books belonging to other children. I looked in one of them and saw beautiful Hindi writing. A maths textbook from the trunk was basic and conventional. There was also a work-book for practice with the numbers from one to ten.

During the short time we were there, another half-dozen boys came in to start work. Some, we were told, were preparing for the sixth or seventh class, because they wanted to go to open school. (In formal education in Delhi classes start at the age of five, so the sixth class is for eleven-year-olds.) All the children there showed a determined concentration over what they were doing; it is moving almost to the point of tears to see a twelve-year-old boy totally committing himself to sounding out letters, or practising basic addition.

Butterflies also runs what it calls the Community Project, a scheme for helping children who live with their families in one particular slum area. Before the scheme started, some of the children would come to contact points, but their parents would not allow them to go to school, because the families needed the money they earned on the streets. Butterflies educators went to try to persuade the parents that education was worthwhile, that their children would eventually earn more if they were allowed to go to school, and that there were economies they, the parents, could make and other ways they could earn extra money. Eventually the educators thought they had found a group who could manage in school, but none of the children had birth certificates, so the schools would not accept them. The relevant department was persuaded to offer to make birth certificates for them, but none of the families could afford to pay the price that was demanded. Finally, in the early 1990s, Butterflies persuaded the Department of Education to require schools to accept all the children who applied, after merely asking their ages. The slum children went to the schools, but after two or three years they began dropping out again; they could not keep up because they had nowhere to read or to do homework. Butterflies then set up special contact points where children could come every day for help with school work and games, and to organise picnics and celebrations. There are now five such contact points, to each of which about thirty children come regularly, and fifty or sixty come occasionally. More than ninety per cent of the children from this area are now going to school and coping with the work.

A special meeting with a dozen children aged between six and twelve was arranged for us. We asked them what they did with Butterflies. Bhaiya comes and does their homework with them, we were told; they go for picnics; they themselves made a space for their class within their community; they organise a sports day; they fight for their own rights, and for other children's rights too; some of them go to the theatre project; two are in the Butterflies Broadcasting Children; a few belong to the Delhi Child Rights Club. They have their own fortnightly Bal Sabha where they arrange activities, discuss how to improve attendance, choose representatives to ask why people aren't coming. They had recently discussed the violations of their rights by the garage owners who took them on as cheap labour; they decided to do street theatre in front of the garages to show the owners and the general public how they felt.

Some of the children also participate in the big monthly Bal Sabha. We asked whether any of them had spoken there.

A girl said she had raised the question of the way girls were teased, something that had already been discussed in the small Bal Sabha. There were many solutions suggested, including street theatre and songs to raise people's awareness of the problem, and a protest march by young girls. This had already made some impression.

Some children go to school in the morning and some in the afternoons, depending on their responsibilities in the home. We asked them what they did when they came home after school, and eight children replied, several of them giving an account of their full day. One girl had to look after her baby sister for part of the day, another had to do the housework. A boy told us he took part in every possible Butterflies activity, and had once used the time between half-past three and four o'clock to collect wood for a celebratory bonfire; we were not to tell his mother because she had sent him out to earn money. Several of the children spent time watching television; all the slum dwellings have televisions because second-hand they cost almost nothing, and it is easy to steal electricity from the power lines. There were two sisters, the elder of whom liked to read story-books, and was already working as a junior educator, teaching the younger children to read and to do sums. She had reached seventh standard in formal education, and was able to teach up to third or fourth. Her sister, who was also a lively talker, said she did not want to be like her; she liked to discuss things, and she liked to help out other people, but she was not interested in formal education, only in playing, theatre and picnics.

We asked the children whether they preferred school or Butterflies, and got an overwhelming shout of "Butterflies" as a reply. We asked why, and the replies illustrated the differences between formal and non-formal education.

At school, we were told, they study and have no time for anything else. When they come to Butterflies they can do whatever they are interested in.

At school there are no outings and there is no fun.

At school the teacher beats them, and the children fight and the teachers don't stop them. In Bhaiya's class there is a different atmosphere; they live happily and peacefully together.

Afterwards we were told of two instances of children being injured in school, one in play with other children, and the other as a result of a blow from a teacher. In neither case had the school offered any treatment, and in the second instance Butterflies had brought a case against the teacher. Generally, though, they try to maintain a good relationship with the schools, and to show them how they can better motivate the children if they create a better atmosphere.

These children, who went to school, played games and watched television, who had told us that they hoped to become pilots, social workers, teachers, doctors and who seemed so little different from children in the affluent West, were living in one-room bamboo and plastic shacks with families of up to ten people, had to spend part of each day working to earn money for food and clothing, were often beaten by the police and had nowhere to go, indoors or outside, where they could be alone. They were probably the most fortunate of all the Butterflies children we met.

Evidence of Success

When we had asked Rita, on our first day, what she would describe as success, she had said success is:

(i) when the children trust adults;
(ii) when children are empowered with knowledge and skills to make correct choices and decisions in their lives;
(iii) when children learn to read and write, even though they may get no academic qualifications;
(iv) when they go on to high school and get good jobs.

How far does Butterflies achieve these goals?

Do the children trust adults?

It is an understatement to say that the children trust the Butterflies adults. One child, quoted in the street-children's report, said he had found "a light in the darkness: Bhaiya-Didi who love us, look after us and fight with the police and our employers for us."

Bhaiya and Didi, brother and elder sister, are the titles by which all the staff are known, even Rita Didi, who appears to be regarded by the staff with a respect close to reverence – a respect which seemed to us to be well-deserved.

Butterflies has achieved this level of trust in a world in which, a group of children told me, there are no other adults you can trust except your own parents. In this world not only your teachers and the police may beat you, but also your own father, and any affectionate gesture from a stranger is likely to be a prelude to an approach for sex. When anything is stolen you are likely to be the first suspect, when you ask your employer for payment he may well refuse to pay you and the police demand *hafta* before they will let you work in their area. The so-called Observation Homes, where children are taken by the police when they are removed from the streets, are little better than prisons, and what is more prisons where there is habitual beating from the staff and violence among the inmates.

And yet not only are the Bhaiya-Didi trusted, but also Lynette and I were accepted without question, and when we arrived at Amin's workshop he greeted us with hugs.

This expansive trust did not come easily. To start with Rita and the other educators had to spend weeks on the streets, simply talking to the children who wanted to talk, finding out what they wanted to do, where they wanted help. Now the example of other children makes it easier for newcomers. This trust stems in part from the fact that the street educators are not trying to impose anything on the children; they are simply offering them advice and help and the opportunity to study if they want to. As Ishani said, the trunkful of learning materials is always there, and open, and many of the children choose to study, precisely because no-one is obliging them to do anything.

And it stems in part from the fact that the staff are always listening, rather than instructing. I commented to Claire, towards the end of our visit, that the street educators seemed to remain very much in the background during the children's activities, and she said that this was deliberate. At the Bal Sabha the children sit in a big circle and the adults remain outside it, audience rather than participants. At the IDEC conference in Tokyo, Rita had stressed the importance of proper listening when she described how every evening she had to ask herself, "Did I consult the children? Did I listen to what they were saying? Or did I just hear a little bit and then make my own decisions?"

And it stems in part from the way the staff treat the children with respect; they are not condescended to as recipients of charity, but accorded the dignity of working people who pay for what they are given. Lynette and I attended a staff meeting where the staff were debating on the issue of paying the cost of transport for children who came for the theatre group or *Bal Mazdoor ki Awaz* editorial meetings. The children who came to the office for these meetings were given their bus-fares, but that meant that they were dependent on Butterflies. The staff discussed the consequences of such dependency and came to the following conclusions :

> *Children must contribute to the costs of their activities.*
> *We help children to develop their knowledge and skills.*
> *We never give children money – we may give them a cup of tea and a snack, but that is all.*
> *It is wrong to give a financial incentive. We want children to decide whether to take part or not, not whether they want the money. We will not even give them the bus-fare.*

This apparent severity allows the children to retain a dignity which would otherwise be lost. I offended one boy severely by asking him a question which was misunderstood to imply that I thought he was begging. When I apologised he accepted the apology as settling a matter between equals. Both his offence and his way of accepting my apology showed that he had a proper self-respect.

And finally the Butterflies children trust the Bhaiya-Didis because the Bhaiya-Didis trust them.

Are children are empowered with knowledge and skills to make correct choices and decisions in their lives?

I have already described Amin and Anuj's workshop, and quoted extensively from the *Bal Mazdoor ki Awaz*. The Bal Sabhas have been mentioned, and the way the children bring up issues there and try to find ways of dealing with them. Other projects have included street theatre, protest marches and press conferences. This is by no means all.

The BBC, the Butterflies Broadcasting Children, was started after a workshop supported by the British Council which was aimed at training street children to do their own interviews and make their own programmes. They have recorded some Delhi Child Rights Club programmes for the Gandhi Peace Foundation; they recorded a big press conference where they interviewed and were interviewed by journalists and other media people; they have recorded Bal Sabha; they have an archive of interviews with street educators and community project organisers, and a series of interviews with girls about their particular problems. I had a meeting with them, and they recorded our mutual interviews. Manpreet, writing in *Bal Mazdoor ki Awaz* just after BBC had been founded, gave a list of hopes for the future:

We should have a separate studio of our own and do our own reporting.
I want to become a reporter in BBC if I stay alive.
I want to teach other children in the studio about what we learnt in this workshop.
I look forward to learn more than what I have already learnt.

In amongst the optimism there is the dreadful reminder of the fragility of their hopes – "if I stay alive."

The search for solutions to problems is part of the children's lives. A new one that was threatening during our visit was that the recycling firms that bought the rag-pickers' findings were being obliged to move out of the centre of Delhi, so the children would have no-one to sell to. The children would have to find some other employment.

Their two biggest problems are the violence associated with alcohol and the violence of the police. Their solutions are attempts to raise public awareness of their situation through rallies, street theatre and songs. Butterflies has set up a weekly training session in which educators talk to the police.

The Delhi Child Rights Club includes children from NGOs all over Delhi. We watched a meeting where they sat in circles to discuss what had gone wrong with their latest public relations project. Why, when they set up a special occasion for a public meeting between street children and journalists and politicians, did none of the politicians come? There had been a truck strike which made it difficult to get through the streets, and parliament had only just reconvened, but that was not enough of an explanation. One solution had been to offer to go to visit the Prime Minister, but this offer had not been accepted. A solution suggested for the next time was that they should invite the opposition members first, so that the government ministers would feel obliged to come.

The life of a child on the street is made up of individual projects and solutions to problems. Butterflies helps them to be more ambitious in the former, and more collaborative in the latter.

Do the children learn to read and write?

We saw children taking minutes at meetings. We heard hesitant reading, and saw exercise-books full of writing. We saw the wallpaper, *Bal Mazdoor ki Awaz*, which is written by a team of Butterflies children. We met the children from the Community Programme who had been enabled to return to formal education and make a success of it.

We also heard the inability to write mentioned without criticism when scribes were chosen at Amin and Anuj's workshop, and in the description of the methodology for the Street Children's Report it says, "Those who can write will write, while the others can be recorded and then put on paper by Bhaiya." On the Delhi streets, children are not expected to be able to read and write, and they learn first to depend on their memories.

Nevertheless, the educators estimate that about sixty per cent of the children who come for six months will learn to read and write within that time.

Do the children go on to high school and get good jobs?

Because we became so involved in observing the children as they were when we met them, this question was forgotten until near the end of our visit, when we spoke to Claire for most of an evening. I asked her what happened when the children became fifteen or sixteen, and this was her reply:

It's amazing how resilient these children are as children, and how much energy they've got, and how they deal with everything often in a very positive way. They are able to live for the moment, and when good things happen they're happy, and then the bad things come along and they're sad and then the next good thing comes along and this way they'll survive. What I noticed, particularly the first time I was here, was that when they get to this youth stage you can see the whole thing become more negative. They actually start thinking of their future, and actually what the hell am I going to do and I don't want to be on the street this many years, and what if I wanted to have a family and so on, what's really my life ahead of me.

In '95 there were a number of boys who were working as porters in the bus station, so when I came about three years later they were like now, nineteen, twenty, and a lot of them were still working as porters in the bus station. And I said, "Oh, you're still here," and they said, "Well, actually we got trained in between. We did electrical training and we had this job and that job, but we were paid almost less than we can earn here, and the bosses, they expected you to run round and do everything for them." And they said, "After three months I'd learnt all I had to learn there. So what's the point in staying?"

So for some, I think, once they've got this freedom of living on the street and working, they're actually too used to being self-employed and they find it difficult to have a boss. But the other thing was that these boys, because they were now adults and because they knew everyone in the bus station, suddenly found that they weren't exploited, they weren't badly treated like they had been when they were younger, and so they felt they had quite a good deal working as porters in the bus station. Together with a group of friends they were renting a room, so they weren't living on the street any more.

So some, just by becoming adults, stay in similar work because the conditions are so much better. There are others who are now rickshaw drivers, some who work in restaurants and some others are involved in the food industry. There are some who at a younger age really didn't want to go home, but suddenly change their minds, when they are older, so some have gone back to villages. Some have gone on into further education, and some are now stall-holders, and some, we just don't know where they've gone. It's a mixture.

For Claire, wholly involved in her daily work with the children, going on into further education seems to have been barely worth mentioning. For several of the children we spoke to from the Community Programme, though, who had ambitions to become doctors or teachers, further education was clearly a target. To correct the balance, here are the stories of two individuals who met that target, adapted from autobiographies written for Butterflies.

Two autobiographies

Manoj Singh Rawat was born in the country, in the Kumaon Himalaya. His father died when he was two, and he was sent hither and thither from his grandparents to his uncle and back to his mother. He worked on his uncle's farm and went to school. He was beaten by his uncle, who was an alcoholic, he was beaten at school because his relations could not afford to buy notebooks. When he was nine years old he ran away to Delhi. There he was picked up by the police and put in the Delhi Gate Observation Home. A cousin who lived in Delhi was contacted and paid a bribe to have him released, and he returned home to his mother for a few months before running away again.

When he returned to Delhi he worked for a while at his cousin's food stall, but when he found he could earn better money carrying bags at the Inter-State Bus Station he decided to move there. He had to fight with other children to establish his right to be there, and once that was done he had daily trouble from the police and the licensed porters, who were angry when the children took their work. He made friends, however, and every day they would work between three and five hours to earn enough money for food and movies, and then they would enjoy the rest of the day together, watching movies, playing and swimming in the river. In the winter months they would hire two blankets between a group of six children and all sleep huddled together for warmth.

He soon learnt to gamble, and when his skills improved he gambled with adults as well as with children. "When there was no money in my pockets," he wrote, "I worked as a porter. When I had money I did not go to work. I often did not even notice hunger, as all I wanted to do was gamble. Sometimes I would gamble the whole day with my friends, and when I had the money I would drink also."

The first time I met a street educator was in ISBT [the Inter-State Bus Terminal] in 1988, when I had injured my leg. A week before my friend had told me about a Bhaiya who had come to ISBT and given some children his visiting card, saying they could contact him if they needed help and that he could also help them with study. At that time I told my friend not to trust him, as I thought that they may be coming from Delhi Gate Child Observation Home. But my friend told me he was a nice man.

The day my leg was injured, my friend brought the street educator to meet me. He talked to me nicely and helped take me to the hospital. That time in my heart I felt 'he is a good man.' His name was Morris. We had to return to the hospital 3 or 4 times, after which my leg was OK. During our visits to the hospital we used to talk about my life.

As a group of children we started to meet him every afternoon in a local park. We used to talk about our difficulties, problems and our lives. At that time we talked openly and straightforwardly. We would say anything that came to our minds, whether right or wrong. The teacher had so won our hearts that we used to tell him everything. He listened to us very carefully and would answer our questions.

...

A month after meeting Morris, I met Rita Didi. She came to ISBT to meet our group in the park. First of all she asked our names and where we had come from. Then she asked us about our feelings about living and working in ISBT. We were happy to meet her, to know that someone else was thinking about our lives. We were given her phone number and she told us we could contact her any time in her house.

We continued to have regular discussions with Morris in the park, and sometimes a man called Father Remi would also come. After a few months they started some 'non-formal education (NFE) classes'. Sometimes we attended for reading, writing and playing, but sometimes we didn't as we were busy gambling or watching movies.

...

Six or seven months after we had been meeting together in ISBT, Morris talked to us about meeting some of the other children who they were working with in other parts of Delhi. At the beginning we wondered why we should meet with children in other areas, we were more concerned with our own lives and wanted to sort out the problems in our area. But our street educator said it would be good for us to share our problems and ideas with the other children.

We went to Chandni Chowk with Morris to have a big meeting with other street and working children. This was our first 'Big Bal Sabha'. There were about 30 children and we talked about the problems we faced in our areas (e.g. harassment from the police and porters), as well as about the fighting amongst ourselves.

Sometimes we also visited Butterflies office to meet with Rita Didi, other people, and to have more 'Big Bal Sabha'. When we were there we also had the chance to shower with hot water.

When he was thirteen he worked for a year at the Butterflies restaurant, which had been set up, both to provide good cheap food for the street children themselves, and to give them work experience in catering. He left when he was fourteen because he decided he wanted to study more and aim for a better career than that of cook, waiter or restaurant manager.

For eighteen months he earned good money as a coolie (labourer), an auto-rickshaw driver and in a travel-agent's office. Most of this money went on food, movies, clothes and gambling. He severed his connections with Butterflies, but Rita Didi kept trying to talk to him. Finally he accepted an invitation to visit her at home, but did not answer many of her questions; in spite of this she said she would think about other opportunities for him.

A few months later I was again invited to meet with Rita Didi. She gave me the offer of studying, whilst also working in the Butterflies office. At first I refused. But a few days later I was given the message that the offer was still open if I was interested. That day I thought very carefully about myself. I felt I had the choice of working in ISBT for more money but no good conditions, or I could study for a better life. I decided that it would be better for me to move from the street to improve myself for the future.

On August 4th 1992 [when he was sixteen] I joined the Butterflies office as an office boy. I delivered letters and parcels, bought stationery, made tea and kept the office clean. In the evenings and when I had free time in the days I studied. At nights I slept in the office. At first it was difficult for me to get along with my colleagues, as we didn't understand each other. I felt alone. However, with time things improved, as I got to know people better and as we came to understand each other's ways. After a few months I enjoyed working there.

After 6 months I was enrolled in a Tuition College. This was preparation for me to join the National Open School. I went to College early morning from 7 am to 10 am where we learnt to read and write better. After I would go to the office.

In 1994 I joined the National Open School. I collected books from a centre and started to study in my own time. I was pleased to have the chance to study. However, at first I found it difficult because I had to go straight from class 4 to class 8. Having missed many years of school, I found the subjects quite difficult. I was learning Hindi, English, Accounts, Economics and History.

...

At this time in 1994 Rita Didi and her husband Gerry Pinto also asked me, 'Manoj, why don't you do street educator work?' However, at that time I told Gerry Sir that 'Right now I was not satisfied with my own knowledge. First I need a few more years to learn more, then I would like to do street educator work.' Gerry told me I would be a good street educator as I had my own experience and knowledge from living on the street.

...

In March 1996 I became a street educator.

...

Without Butterflies organisation I don't know where I would be or what I would be doing. Maybe I would be working as an auto-rickshaw driver, or as a licenced porter. Maybe I would still be living on the streets, still gambling my life away. I don't think I would have reached Class 12 in my studies. Nor would I have had the chance to share my experiences with people from other countries.

Now, looking towards my future I hope to start a degree, whilst continuing to do work that is helpful for children.

Ashraf Nias is another street educator who was a street child himself from the age of eleven. He ran away from a dictatorial father and a school where he was beaten and only taught Arabic and Urdu. Like Manoj, he worked in ISBT as a porter.

I used to enjoy my life on the streets, especially the freedom. This was perhaps because I was brought up in a very strict family. It was a patriarchal family where my father decided everything. In contrast, here on the streets I had full freedom, there was nobody to direct my activities. I was free to do anything I wanted to.

However, despite the freedom, we working children faced lots of problems in ISBT, especially from the porters with licences. These porters used to beat us and take our money. We were helpless as we had to stay there and then they would beat us more. We children also faced a lot of problems from the police who beat us regularly. At night we did not sleep outside in the park as there were many adults who would harass us. So we used to sleep inside the ISBT building. However, in the middle of the night when we would be sleeping the police would come and beat us. If we would give them money they would stop, otherwise not. Local goondas (gangsters) also used to take money from us.

Whilst living, working, playing and sleeping on the streets I met Rita Didi, Father Remi and Morris Bhaiya. However, my street experience taught me not to trust anybody. My experience was that adults talked to us nicely when they wanted to get something from us (e.g. our money, their own sexual satisfaction). So at first I didn't trust these street educators. I used to meet them and speak to them, but I wouldn't go anywhere with them. In those days, Bhaiya was planning to take us for a picnic to Pragati Maidan, but very few boys actually went with him.

When Rita Didi started coming to ISBT regularly we became very close to her. Her personality had a charisma which attracted us. Whenever she used to call, we would all immediately go to her. One of the main reasons for this was that ever since I started living on the streets, she was the first person who had spoken to me as if I was dear to her. She addressed me as "son". I used to look forward to meet her. Rita Didi was the first person to ask us about the problems we faced during and prior to our street life. No one had ever spoken to us so passionately about our challenges on the street, and wanted to know who beat or abused us. While speaking to her we used to get a feeling that all our problems were hers as well.

...

Ever since I attached myself with Butterflies there has been a lot of changes in my life and thoughts. For the first time I got to know that I have some rights which are denied to me. I started attending Bal Sabha regularly. Butterflies always gave us the space to express our ideas and to act on these ideas. The educators and we had equal rights. We were always encouraged to come together and to make our own decisions. Bhaiya and Didi were "guides" who encouraged our full participation.

Whenever we faced problems we would come together to discuss everything in a meeting. Through Bal Sabha we learnt that we ourselves have the solutions for all our problems.

...

The problems and difficulties I faced while living on the streets are still a painful memory. Street life is such where no one is one's own except perhaps the peer group. Adults snatch away money; police thrash us without reason; adults and shop-keepers who are around lure us to borrow money and to satisfy their own needs. The police nab us for the crimes we have never

135

committed and also make us clean the police station or send us to remand homes or observation homes.

However, the Butterflies street educators gave us much support. If ever we faced any problems we were encouraged to share them and Bhaiya/Didi would always fully support us in finding solutions. For example they would talk with the police to try to stop their harassment.

Once our NFE [non-formal education] class was taking place in a park near ISBT. Three or four police officers came with the licensed porters and police inspector in charge. The police did not want us to study there, nor the porters wanted us to work in the area. However, our Bhaiya "Brother Morris" explained about our programme and showed our ID cards. Despite Morris's arguments the police still did not want us to hold our classes in the park. The police informed us that to study in the park we needed permission from the higher NDMC [New Delhi Municipal Corporation] authorities. Along with Morris our struggle to be allowed to study in the park was taken to the higher authorities. We continued to meet Bhaiya and study in the park.

...

I spent three months in one of the Observation Homes which I consider as some of the worst days of my life. There the older inmates ruled, they would thrash and abuse anybody they wanted to. One doesn't even get proper food in such homes. While I was there, I witnessed the brutal torture of two boys who tried to escape. Till today I find it difficult to narrate this incident, nor can I forget their physical state. They were thrashed so brutally that the skin of their feet came off. All of us were told that we would share a similar fate if we ever tried to flee from the home. The same legs which would be used to flee would be broken.

Ashraf goes on to relate other horrors from his later experience as a street educator, involving violence and sexual abuse. He also tells of the lack of support from shopkeepers.

The local shop-keepers are also against us. These shops have helper boys of 10-15 years who probably work for 14 to 16 hours a day at very low wages and in unhygienic conditions. Our contact with such boys poses threat to the owners. After being with us, the children become aware of their rights and demand their wage or time which earlier would never even occur to them. These boys are mainly from villages who come through brokers to the city. Frequently, they have never been paid their due wages. In such situation they are like bonded labourers. Our non-formal education classes are always full of discussion on child rights and workers' rights and our children are given the skills to protect themselves from being cheated. Since the employers do not want to lose such cheap labourers they consider it to be a loss on their part if the children come to us for studies. The employers and rag-picker buyers also see our classes as time-wasting activities, since the children who come to us do not spend that time in collecting rags which in turn affects his income.

Our endeavour is to co-relate our education programme with children's work and income, to enable the child to negotiate for a better wage with the employer. No wonder that shop-keepers not only are against us but also deliberately create problems for us.

Ashraf also works as a facilitator with the Delhi Child Rights Club.

I have learnt a lot from my experience in this club. I believe if children are given a platform to express themselves they can do anything. DCRC has done lots of programmes and one of them was held in November. The whole programme was planned by children. This programme would have been a revelatory experience for those who believe that children are not capable of making their own decisions.

Today at this juncture of my life when I take stock of what life has given me in these 25 years, I find that there are certain milestones in my life. ... From being an object that was looked after, protected and directed when I became involved with Butterflies whilst working on the streets I became a citizen who was capable of self-care, self-protection and participation. I know I would have not achieved so much if I had not been associated with Butterflies. Butterflies played a very important role in shaping my life. Life has taught me the values of self-expression, decision-making and collective ownership. Today I feel, realising my rights and sharing responsibility on the street have groomed me to be an adult who is committed to ensure participation of children not only outside the family but also in the family.

Had I been given the right to make choices and take decisions at the early stages of my life, I would have never left home. And precisely for this reason I further believe that participation from early stages of life is possible and is the only radical option for making today's children effective citizens of tomorrow.

I intend to continue to work with children to get their rights and to help them to solve their problems for all of my life. I specially want to work for street and working children, because I know the problems as I have experienced them myself when I was a street child. I know the life on streets is tough, painful and very lonely, and therefore I want to be a friend of these children.

Other Activities

Butterflies is not only an organisation of street educators. As well as the activities I have touched on, they provide children with ID cards which give them a small measure of security; they run a Childline service with a crisis centre where children can be housed until solutions to their problems can be found; they publish cartoon books about social problems in India seen from the point of view of two children; they produce a quarterly journal on child rights called *My Name is Today*; they nurture international contacts; and they publish research.

What Lynette and I saw and heard in Delhi made it plain that the work of the street educators is successful, even against extraordinary odds, but it cannot always succeed, and sometimes it cannot begin soon enough. This is what Vikky, who was selling chu-chu toys in Connaught Place, told the children who were researching for the Street Children's Report:

> *The police come and take away our stuff. It is very difficult to get it out and I often have to pay Rs. 500/- to get it out.*
>
> *I used to study in Bombay. My mother died when there were riots in January after the Babri Masjid fell. The house was burnt as well, and our father brought us to Delhi. Papa has not got a good job yet. We both work and so the house runs. My younger brother also works.*
>
> *When the police beats us up, people nearby don't do anything to help and don't say anything either.*
>
> *I should have been studying right now. But how can I? How will the house run? If the Government wants to educate me, it will have to give my dad a good job, so that he can send me to school.*
>
> *I have lost everything by working, most of all my childhood.*

Vikky was nine years old.

Conclusion

I wrote in my introduction that I hoped to find evidence that non-authoritarian education was suitable for children even from backgrounds like those described in this book. What I have seen, heard and read has led me to form a stronger opinion.

I discovered, for instance, that the various methods I saw practised were not chosen particularly because the children came from hard backgrounds. David Wills, the Quaker, put it like this:

> ... *the one thing needful was that we should maintain 'not only with our lips, but in our lives' an attitude of unswerving, unconditional, unshakable affection.* **Not because this would 'cure' them or bring about some preconceived human end of our own, but because this was what was required of us by divine injunction.** [My emphasis.]

To put it in secular terms, you do not use the non-authoritarian approach because it is a humane way of encouraging children to lead better lives, but because it is their right to be treated in this way. The fact that this results in responsible, caring members of society is a by-product, not the essential aim.

It has to be acknowledged that non-authoritarian education is widely misunderstood and therefore mistrusted. The conventional beliefs are that, without rules and punishments to govern their behaviour, young people will be idle, violent, promiscuous, self-indulgent, rebellious, aimless and vicious and that children who are not forced to learn what society has laid down for them will learn nothing. I have seen enough to show that these beliefs are groundless. If any children were to be failed by non-authoritarian education, it would surely be the children described in this book. Many of them had faced, or indeed were still facing, abuse, starvation, rape, torture and an ever-present risk of death.

Throughout the book I have been largely concerned with the positive changes that had been effected in the children's lives, so a few reminders of the severity of their difficulties may be necessary. In the Chicago gangs, some of the girl members had to submit to routine multiple rape. Thirteen-year-olds were given guns to defend their territory, and killed each other on the streets. In some of the Observation Homes in Delhi, children were imprisoned, and tortured if they tried to escape. Outside the Observation Homes they were frequently beaten by the police. Before they came to Moo Baan Dek, some children had suffered so badly that they were only invited to go to lessons after three years of play and therapeutic activities; a few had been treated so violently that they had suffered brain damage.

Many of the children I met had, for various reasons, only just been able to survive what they had endured. If it were natural for any children to develop a hatred and mistrust of adults, these children would certainly have done so.

Non-authoritarian education is thought to stem from a sentimental belief in the goodness of human nature. I saw ample evidence of responsibility, concern for others and a desire to make the world a better place in children whose backgrounds were stark and brutal. This is not sentimentality, it is fact.

Non-authoritarian was the word I chose from my list of possible names for the kind of education exemplified in this book – progressive, free, democratic, child-centred and liberal were the others – but none of them seem adequate to describe the approaches of the educators I met. Pibhop and Rajani Dhongchai, the founders of Moo Baan Dek, were aiming to "arrange the environment or external factors that would cultivate wisdom and kindness into the human heart while reducing ignorance and vice, so that life is led to its ultimate aim; being in harmony with nature, and having *wisdom* as life's guide and *kindness* as its inspiration." Rita Panicker, of Butterflies, had to struggle against her upbringing every day to make sure that she consulted the children properly. Her reward was the children's trust. David Wills, from the Barns Hostel, said, "First and foremost and all the time the children must feel themselves to be loved."

Progressive? Free? Child-centred? Democratic? Liberal? Non-authoritarian? The words are trivial in this kind of context. Bertrand Russell thought true education was characterised by reverence, but even "reverent education" would be an incomplete description.

At all the places I have described, children were not merely helped to deal with their problems, they were helped to discover their own potential. I do not only mean potential as educationalists use it, in the sense of academic ability; I include that sense, but I also mean social potential, potential for self-respect, the children's potential to assert their own rights and to play a full role in their communities.

The Delhi Child Rights Club organised major events for themselves. In Chicago, student Ada Rivera was learning to say, "OK, we're not going to get pushed around," and Marvin Garcia, the principal, was saying, "We're trying to help people to take control of their lives, and live their lives with dignity." In the council at Moo Baan Dek students sometimes overrule adults. The boys at the Barns Hostel ran it themselves for eight months, and the oldest of them was thirteen.

"The finest type of citizen," said David Wills, "is he who obeys no law blindly out of an unthinking respect for authority or fear of penalties; it is he whose conduct is based on a rational understanding of why a given type of behaviour is desirable, and who will persist in that type of behaviour whatever the consequences to himself."

It seems extraordinary that any educational system should consciously set out to prevent children from taking control of their lives and from making their own decisions, should force them to obey "out of an unthinking respect for authority or fear of penalties." And it seems extraordinary that we should have to look to such extreme examples as the ones I have been describing if we are to learn any better. How can it not be obvious that children and young people must be allowed to live their lives with dignity, to base their conduct on a rational understanding of why a given type of behaviour is desirable, to overrule adults when the adults are mistaken?

The first criterion for success with children who have suffered as those in this book have done is simply emotional and physical survival. Rita Panicker said that other things followed only when the children trusted the adults. Pibhop and Rajani Dhongchai said that emotional scars would never heal in an authoritarian environment, but must have an atmosphere of freedom, love and warmth. David Wills said that what was needed was "a relationship such that, however much the child might wound his own self-esteem, he could not damage the esteem in which the adults held him."

Even children who have suffered as these children have done want to learn so badly that they are prepared to make great sacrifices to get the opportunity. Ex-gang-members in Chicago lose a social network and a high income and run a serious risk of retaliation. Street children in Delhi give up valuable working time when every rupee represents food, clothes or shelter.

Against backgrounds like these, requirements about school uniforms and punishments for breaching trivial rules seem absurdities. Anyone who sees how these children succeed without such conventional repression will wonder why on earth so many people think it necessary elsewhere. Children desperately want to learn, and yet conventional education still manages to discourage them to such an extent that in the end teachers have to resort to coercion.

Freedom, trust, warmth and love should be regarded as basic rights; when they are so regarded, the results are dignity, responsibility and concern for other people, and children learn because they enjoy learning and understand its purpose.

I have seen evidence that this is true for some of the most disadvantaged children in the world. Children from secure backgrounds will manage somehow under almost any system. The children for whom non-authoritarian education matters most are the deprived, the down-trodden, the deserted and the desperate. For the rich, such education is suitable; for the poor, it is essential.

Appendix

Addresses

Dr. Pedro Albizu Campos Puerto Rican High School
2739 West Division Street
Chicago, IL 60622
USA

Moo Baan Dek
Latya-Srisawat Road
Kanchanaburi 71190
Thailand
Internet: http://www.ffc.or.th/mbd

Butterflies Programme of Street and Working Children
U4, First Floor
Green Park Extension
New Delhi 110 016
India

References

David Wills and the Barns Hostel:

Wills, W.D. (1945), *The Barns Experiment,*London, Allen and Unwin.
Wills, W.D. (1960), *Throw Away Thy Rod*, London, Gollancz.

Moo Baan Dek:

Cowhey, Ellen and Udomittipong, Pibop (1997), *Real Life at Moo Baan Dek.*Bangkok, Foundation for Children.
Dhongchai, Pibhop and Rajani (undated), *Children Village School.* Bangkok, Foundation for Children.

Butterflies:

Sen, Ishani (1999), *"Children's Participation in Evaluating Butterflies NFE Programme"*, in *My Name is Today*, Vol. VII, No 1 and 2, New Delhi, Butterflies, pp. 15 ff.

Sen, Ishani and O'Kane, Clare (2001), *In Search of Fair Play: Street and Working Children Speak about their Rights*, New Delhi, Butterflies in Association with Mosaic Books.

Papers prepared for Butterflies:

Street Children's Report (undated)

Nias, Mohd. Ashraf (2000), *Street Life and Street Work Experiences.*

Rawat, Manoj Singh (2000), *Reflections on my Childhood, Street Life and Experiences with Butterflies.*